THE ZEN KITCHEN

不許葷酒山門

'Those who have eaten noxious food or drunk alcohol may not enter the temple'

– ENGRAVED ON STONE PILLARS OUTSIDE ZEN TEMPLE GATES

THE ZEN KITCHEN

ADAM LIAW

WITH ASAMI FUJITSUKA

hachette
AUSTRALIA

CONTENTS

For our daughter Anna, who made writing this book easy in her own way.

INTRODUCTION

The Japanese approach to food is one we might all admire. Simultaneously respectful, appreciative, enthusiastic and practical, it's an approach that has produced one of the world's greatest cuisines and one that is simple to cook, healthy, delicious and hugely varied.

It's done this not through some happy accident that saw good produce meet good cooks, but through centuries of forging a strong connection between food and people. To understand Japanese food is not just to know how to cook it, but it is also to understand what it represents.

In Japan, food is something used to celebrate, to educate. It's more than just a part of Japanese culture, it is a totality of Japanese culture presented in its most tangible form.

This is my fifth cookbook, and while my earlier books have all included many Japanese recipes, this is the first book I've written solely devoted to Japanese cuisine. In writing it, I wrestled with the best way to communicate what Japanese food truly is, not just in the mechanics of how to make it, but to put it in context of the culture it's entwined with so completely.

Ultimately I decided that the best way to do that was the way most Japanese people learn about their own cuisine, which is not through the rote learning of recipes and measurements, but through the stories and idioms that tie culture and cooking together, for truly neither could exist without the other. We can learn as much about food from a story or proverb as we can from a measurement or method. Often more.

In 2016 the Japanese government appointed me to serve as an official Goodwill Ambassador for Japanese Cuisine. It was the first time that honour had been bestowed outside Japan, and one I was humbled to receive. The responsibility in this role, however, is a simple one, as within Japanese cuisine there is much goodwill to share.

Throughout this book, through each recipe, picture, instruction and sentence, I will be guiding you through how to cook, eat and understand Japanese food. The kind of food my family, and thousands like it, eat every day. The kind of food that has made Japan one of the longest-lived, healthiest, and most food-loving nations on Earth.

Itadakimasu.

A YEAR OF EATING

Japan is a country of four seasons, and although that simple fact may seem common enough, it's what Japan does with those seasons that is truly special.

I have never experienced another country where the seasons have such a profound impact. It's not just about the weather that the seasons bring, although that certainly changes as well, but in the way they affect seemingly every aspect of daily life.

In terms of food we tend to think of seasonality as relating mostly to the availability of ingredients, and while that's certainly important, in Japan seasonality goes much deeper than just what's in the shops.

An understanding of seasonal ingredients is common knowledge. The youngest child will have a favourite fish for each of spring, summer, autumn and winter. The dishes themselves will also be different in their style, composition and even seasoning. Summer foods will be slightly more salty to encourage drinking, and vinegared dishes will have more piquancy to stimulate appetite. As the season moves to autumn, similar dishes will take on slightly more savoury characteristics in place of the sourness. Winter and spring dishes are less heavily salted than those served in summer. From season to season, even the plates and bowls used for serving food will change, as they are chosen to communicate an impression of each season through colour, shape, material or motif.

THE IMPORTANCE OF QUALITY

Every town or region in Japan has a specialty – an ingredient or dish that they feel they grow or cook better than anywhere else on Earth. Tuna from Oma, peaches from Yamanashi, rice from Niigata or ramen from Fukuoka – it sometimes seems like Japan is a nation where everyone seems to be striving for perfection in one field or another.

Heavily marbled wagyu beef from areas like Matsuzaka, Hida and Kobe are peerless in flavour and texture. The same could be said for the kurobuta pork from Kagoshima and the delicious Agu breed from Japan's most pork-loving region, Okinawa. The buttery flavour and texture of Nagoya cochin chicken would rival the finest Bresse birds from France.

The thing about quality is you have to decide what it means to you: increased satisfaction or increased desire? When food is high quality and delicious we don't need to eat as much to be satisfied, although we may want to eat more. To push past contentment for the sheer sport of it seems indulgent at best, and obscene at its worst.

The appreciation of food is not an ever-increasing scale. Being satisfied with one portion of food does not mean we'll be twice as satisfied with two. A rich piece of wagyu beef is an exquisite delicacy at 120 grams, but eat a 350g steak by yourself and you might wish you hadn't. Japanese food prizes quality over quantity, and that is fundamental to its enjoyment.

A CULTURE OF FOOD AND HEALTH

For an ancient cuisine, the Japanese diet addresses many of the challenges that affect how we eat today. It's fast to prepare, healthy, created simply from very few ingredients, and interweaves culture and food in a way that gives greater meaning to each meal beyond just a fuel to keep us going, a tool to quiet the kids, or a quick-fix to a flatter summer stomach.

It's hard to argue with one of the healthiest cuisines in the world, and one that has made the Japanese among the longest-lived people on the planet. The Japanese diet embodies many of the points that modern science asks of us in order to eat well. It relies less on red meat than most Western diets, focusing instead on fish and vegetables. It contains fermented foods for digestive health through simple pickles such as Nukazuke (page 18), which are eaten with almost every meal. Rice, although central to the cuisine, is served as a separate element to other dishes, meaning that it is very easy to reduce the amount of refined carbohydrates eaten with your meal, as many Japanese people do these days. Wholegrain rice mixes like the one on page 52 are also hugely popular, boosting the fibre of a bowl of rice as well as providing a delicious flavour.

One of the most attractive and reasonable aspects of the Japanese diet is its moderation. Although vegetables form the bulk of the diet, vegetarianism and veganism is relatively uncommon. While sweets are a much-loved treat and sugar is a necessary seasoning, they are rightly considered only parts of a much broader cuisine. The Japanese diet doesn't rely on restrictive exclusions to communicate a message of good health. Good health is inherent to the cuisine. It is a true love of food, wary of the trappings of gluttony or breathless excess.

If you were to design a perfect diet based on what modern science tells us today, it might look a lot like the way Japan has been eating for centuries. But the appeal of Japanese food goes far further than the clinical sterility of science.

Stories of food and health and their role in a long and happy life are woven through lore and culture so that the lessons of the kitchen teach Japanese children not just how to cook and eat, but how to live well. This kind of education is so important, as it affects everything from saving a few minutes each day through efficient kitchen technique, to a lifetime of healthy eating that's also enjoyable, convivial and shared with those you love.

This book isn't a health or diet book. Yet Japanese cuisine has had health at its core long before 'health' had any connections to being skinny. You might well look at Japanese cuisine as a manual for living. It touches every aspect of life – relationships, money, politics, manners and, of course, health is a part of it.

When you cook the dishes from this book, try to look beyond just the recipe, as each one is a part of a bigger cultural picture. A piece of grilled fish can be just a quick dinner, but it can also be an act of kindness, a philosophy of health, a lesson in patience, a chance to share a story, and a window into another way of thinking.

THE FIVE PREPARATION METHODS OF JAPANESE COOKING

There are five classic preparation methods in Japanese cuisine – grilling, stewing, deep-frying, steaming and raw. Each requires some discussion and each is slightly different from its Western equivalent.

GRILLING
(焼く, *yaku*)
in Japanese cuisine encompasses a number of different forms. In Western cooking we might think of pan-frying as distinct from barbecuing over open coals, and putting something under an overhead grill as a different style of cooking again. In Japanese cuisine the term *yaku* encompasses all of them, and a simple piece of salmon, for example, can be cooked in the *shioyaki* or salt-grilled style (page 122) in a frying pan, over coals or under a grill. The results will differ, but the goal is the same – warm and tender fish inside with a lightly browned, toasty exterior.

STEWING
(煮る, *niru*)
is all about mastering the amount of liquid needed to produce a particular result. In some dishes it may involve boiling in a lot of liquid for a soupy product, as for Shabu-shabu (page 90) and Oden (page 197), and in others it may mean stewing or simmering in just enough liquid to create a concentrated seasoning, enhancing the flavour of nearly dry dishes like Carrot and Lotus Root Kinpira (page 201) or Braised Tuna (page 147).

DEEP-FRYING
(揚げる, *ageru*)
is quite different to its role in Western cooking. A crisp coating is not always the goal for deep-fried Japanese foods. Dishes like Agedashi Tofu (page 192) or Barbarian Salmon (page 138) use deep-frying as a process to ultimately achieve a silky texture after the deep-fried ingredients are soaked in a seasoned broth. Even for the classic tempura the indicator of excellence is not the crispiness of the coating, but the delicate perfection of the steam-cooked interior. Oiliness is avoided and many Japanese deep-fried dishes are served on folded paper. The paper is used not to soak up oil, quite the opposite, it is used to show how little oil has been absorbed by the food.

STEAMING
(蒸す, *musu*)
is a delicate cooking method that involves using steam at 100°C to gently cook ingredients for dishes like Snapper Chirimushi (page 135), Chicken and Prawn Chawanmushi (page 153), or Steamed Pork with Sesame Sauce (page 150). When steaming ingredients, care must be taken to avoid the steam forming droplets of water that can dilute and potentially spoil a dish. The steaming of rice is done in a pot, not a steamer, but it is a perfect example of how this method of cooking can be controlled. Rather than just boiling rice until it is tender, a combination of absorption and steaming is needed to produce perfectly textured Japanese rice: plump, flavourful and separate grains with just enough stickiness to be picked up with chopsticks. A full explanation can be found on page 52.

RAW
(生, *nama*),
the fifth preparation method, may at first glance appear to be the absence of cooking, but it is in fact a fascinating and nuanced cooking method in its own right. Japan's most famous dish, sushi (page 68), is little more than seasoned rice with a raw ingredient placed on top, but the artistry of the chef is needed to ensure that ingredient is selected at its best, handled and prepared so as not to spoil its natural flavour, sliced to create a harmonious texture and presented in a manner that is appealing. Even the simple process of pickling (pages 17–23) can create dishes that are raw, but which through seasoning and careful preparation result in an ingredient transformed into a dish that exhibits its best flavour.

KITCHEN EQUIPMENT

Many of the tools used in Japanese cuisine may seem quite different from those in your average Western kitchen, but they serve largely the same functions as stuff you probably already have. To get started cooking Japanese cuisine, you really don't need to rush out to get any new equipment, but as you cook more and more Japanese food it may be worth investing in some of these items.

1 SAUCEPANS
OF VARYING SIZE
The size of the saucepan you use is important for the success of many stewed or simmered dishes. Use a saucepan that is too large and you may need to add too much liquid, diluting the flavour of the dish. Use a saucepan that's too small, and ingredients may not cook evenly.

2 RICE COOKER
You'll find a rice cooker at the centre of every Japanese kitchen. They are used both for cooking rice and for hygienically keeping cooked rice warm and at the ready for any meal. You can make great rice in any heavy pot, but a rice cooker makes the whole process very easy.

3 FISH SCALER
AND TWEEZERS
With so much of Japanese cuisine involving fish, these simple tools are very useful. While your fishmonger can scale whole fish and pinbone fillets for you, there will always be occasions when it makes more sense to do it yourself.

4 TRAYS AND BOWLS
FOR PREPARATION
These are the most used items in our kitchen. Care in preparation is the key to Japanese cuisine, and having specific containers for this task is fundamental to good kitchen craft. You can't cook well if you're carrying ingredients across the kitchen in your hands, or on the flat of a knife, or just leaving cut ingredients on the cutting board, crowding yourself into a corner with each stroke of the blade.

5 JAPANESE GRATER
These graters are available from Japanese grocers and are very useful for finely grating ingredients like daikon (for *daikon-oroshi*, see page 125), ginger and garlic. If you don't have one, you can use a rasp grater or the very finest perforations on a box grater, but it will take longer and the results won't be quite as good. While metal graters are best, they can also be made from bamboo or plastic.

6 COOKING CHOPSTICKS
If you're confident with your chopstick ability, cooking chopsticks give you much more control than tongs or spatulas. Cooking chopsticks range from thicker, sturdier types that can be used in high heat, to very fine metal or wooden chopsticks used for the placement and arrangement of food for serving.

7 PICKLING CROCK
Pickles are a part of almost any Japanese meal (see pages 16 to 23) and most families will make many of their own pickles. A pickling crock like the one pictured on pages 6–7 is a nice tool to have, but you can easily use other lidded plastic containers or press-seal bags to make your own pickles.

8 DROP LIDS
Drop lids are crucial to ensuring simmered foods cook and absorb seasoning evenly. Rather than sitting on top of a saucepan's rim, the drop lid sits inside, directly on top of the ingredients, weighing them down and keeping steam and heat around them, while letting moisture evaporate from the gaps between the edge of the lid and the side of the pot. You can find them at Japanese grocers, or you can improvise a kind of cartouche from a sheet of aluminium foil, folded to double thickness and crumpled around the edges to the appropriate size.

9 MISO STRAINER

Miso strainers are used to dissolve miso paste into stock or water to make miso soup. The process is described on pages 80 to 83. The strainer catches any chunks of soybean, grain or pieces of bran, while allowing the miso to be evenly distributed through the soup. If you don't have a miso strainer, you can dissolve the miso by stirring it in a ladle held just under the surface of the soup.

10 STOVETOP FISH GRILL

These fish grills can be used over a gas stove and do a decent job of recreating the flavour of grilling over hot coals without the inconvenience. They produce a strong, radiation and convection heat different from the conduction heat of a frying pan or barbecue. You can get them from Japanese grocers but if you don't have one, just follow the methods on pages 122 to 125 for grilling fish on a frying pan or barbecue, or in an oven.

11 FLAT STRAINER

Used often in conjunction with a huge tub-like Japanese sink, a flat strainer is for washing and draining large or delicate ingredients. You could substitute a wire draining rack or large colander instead.

12 MORTAR AND PESTLE

The difference between a Japanese mortar and pestle and similar tools in other cuisines is that the ceramic Japanese mortars are made more for grinding than pounding. They're the perfect tool for grinding sesame seeds, but you can use an ordinary granite mortar and pestle instead.

13 WOODEN RICE TUB

The process of making sushi rice (page 68) involves tipping freshly cooked rice into one of these tubs and seasoning it with a mixture of vinegar, salt and sugar, separating the grains with a paddle while the rice is vigorously fanned to cool it and evaporate excess moisture. Get one of these if you feel you'll be making a lot of sushi, but otherwise any wide bowl or tray will do just as well.

14 JAPANESE KNIVES

Japanese knives can be of exceptional quality, but they also require some training to use. The single-sided sharpening of many higher-end knives requires a different cutting motion to ordinary double-sided sharpening, and blades made from blue or carbon steel will need much more maintenance than a standard stainless steel blade. For ordinary home cooking, you don't need to invest in expensive new knives. Just make sure the ones you already have are razor sharp.

15 EARTHENWARE POT

A large, communal earthenware pot may seem like an unnecessary addition but I think it's one of the most important pieces of equipment in a Japanese kitchen. For dishes cooked at the table like Soy Milk Nabe (page 94), a simple earthenware dish is far more pleasant to cook and eat from than an industrial metal pot. Think of it as the centrepiece of a winter family meal.

16 PORTABLE STOVE

Using a portable stove is a lovely way to cook. Shared eating is one thing, but for dishes like Shabu-shabu (page 90), and Sukiyaki (page 93), cooking at the table is crucial to their enjoyment. Gas-powered, electric and induction types are available from Asian grocers. If you buy an induction model, it's useful to buy a separate metal induction plate that can transfer heat to an earthenware pot.

17 WIRE MESH SCOOP

For nabe-style dishes that contain meat, a fine wire mesh scoop is used to skim any scum that forms on the surface of the dish. This can be done with a shallow spoon, but the mesh makes it much more efficient.

JAPANESE INGREDIENTS

One of the best things about Japanese cuisine is that it uses so few ingredients. With just the six basic seasonings of soy sauce, mirin, sake, sugar and rice vinegar in the pantry, and some miso in the fridge, you can make just about any Japanese dish you can think of.

13 だし昆布 道南産真昆布 鍋ものに一本！使いやすい

14 有機あわせ 土づくりからはじめた味噌づくり ／ 無添加 一流好み 国産大豆・国産米・国産塩100％使用 ／ 吟醸 信州一味噌

15 新潟県産 こしひかり

16 CHO DANG 연두부 SOFT TOFU 日本軟豆腐 Weight:300g

17 漬物用 いりぬか 味よく漬かる 800g

18 150 本生 わさび ワンタッチ・チューブ

19 藻塩

1 MIRIN

Mirin is a rice wine used to add sweetness and gloss to many dishes, along with a touch of savoury umami. Much thicker in texture and darker in colour than sake, and with a much sweeter flavour, one cannot be substituted for the other.

2 COOKING SAKE

Cooking sakes are produced as a mixture of traditionally fermented sake and distilled alcohol. This gives them a milder flavour and lower acidity than drinking sakes, which can be very useful for cooking. The alcohol helps to carry flavours through a dish. There is no need to buy drinking-quality sake for cooking, as the cheaper cooking varieties will serve their purpose perfectly well. Cooking sake is available from Asian grocers for just a few dollars.

3 SOY SAUCE

Soy sauce is the most popular seasoning in Japanese cuisine, used for its salty-savoury umami taste. There are many varieties, from nearly colourless 'white' versions to thick, strongly flavoured dark sauces (*koikuchi*). By far the most popular and widely used is the standard light soy sauce (*usukuchi*). Brands will vary in their flavour and quality, so try to buy soy sauce that is specified as naturally brewed. Soy sauces that are not specified as naturally brewed can be mixtures of chemical flavour enhancers and colourings, whereas brewed versions will always be the real thing.

4 POTATO STARCH

Potato starch, the most common starch used in Japanese cuisine, is used as a coating for fried foods like Agedashi Tofu (page 192), or as a thickening agent for dishes such as Salmon Ankake (page 141). Cornflour is a good substitute.

5 SALAD OIL

'Salad oil' is the Japanese term given to the blended vegetable oils used for much of Japanese cooking. Neutral in flavour, a simple vegetable oil is fine for cooking most Japanese foods, although I prefer to use grapeseed oil for salads as it has a less oily mouth feel.

6 SUGAR

Sugar and mirin are the two main sweet seasonings in Japanese cooking. The two are often used in combination, sugar providing a clean sweetness while mirin also provides gloss and a light umami flavour.

7 JAPANESE MAYONNAISE

Japanese mayonnaise has a creamier texture and more savoury flavour than many Western mayonnaises. Its low acidity makes it a fantastic complement to many dishes from fried chicken to teriyaki.

8 RICE VINEGAR

Rice vinegar is the main source of sourness and astringency in Japanese food. True rice vinegars will often have a strong umami flavour caused by the fermentation of the rice, while cheaper grain vinegars flavoured with rice may be milder. Both may be used, but it is necessary to understand the difference.

9 SESAME OIL

Toasted sesame oil is very commonly used in Japanese cuisine as a flavouring, adding a toasty and nutty aroma to many dishes. Although cold-pressed sesame oils are used for frying tempura in the south of Japan, the toasted varieties are used much more sparingly, as their strong flavour may overwhelm some dishes.

10 NORI

Used in everything from sushi and salads to ramen and tempura, nori sheets are extremely useful, providing a toasty seaweed flavour that can be enhanced by wafting a sheet over an open flame. Nori sheets should not be confused with aonori, which are the dried, bright green seaweed flakes often scattered over dishes like *okonomiyaki* and *takoyaki*.

11 SHICHIMI TOGARASHI

This seven-spice chilli has no specific recipe, and many different varieties exist. Common ingredients include chilli powder, nori flakes, orange rind, black and white sesame seeds, sansho (a relative of Sichuan pepper) and hemp seeds. While providing a mild heat, shichimi togarashi is also used for its spicy citrus fragrance, as an aromatic topping for soups or noodle dishes, and as a colourful garnish.

12 GREEN TEA POWDER

Japanese green tea powder is a very finely ground powder of tea leaves specially prepared to preserve their vibrant green colour. You cannot substitute other varieties of green teas, as they will differ in flavour and colour. It's used for making formal, highly bitter tea and is a popular ingredient in desserts. It can also be ground with salt as a dip for fried foods such as tempura.

13 KOMBU

Kombu is dried kelp that is used widely throughout Japanese cuisine for its savoury umami taste. One of the most popular uses is for making stocks such as *ichiban dashi* (page 30), an integral building block for Japanese food.

14 MISO

Miso is a paste made from fermenting steamed soybeans, sometimes with other grains such as barley or rice. There are many varities of miso, ranging from light 'sweet' misos that are lower in salt and contain a higher proportion of grains other than soybeans, through to dark red misos made entirely from soybeans. While it's commonly used for soup, miso is incredibly versatile. It can be used as a seasoning or as a medium for pickling or curing.

15 JAPANESE RICE

Japanese short-grain rice varieties such as koshihikari and yumepirika are perfect for serving with Japanese food. Cooked well they are plump, glossy and slightly sticky with a malty and slightly sweet flavour. Refer to page 52 for how to cook rice.

16 TOFU

Made from soybean milk set with magnesium salts, tofu can range from a delicate curd to dense firm cakes. It can also be grilled, fried or flavoured with vegetables. When handling tofu, it's important to manage the amount of liquid retained by the tofu as that will dilute flavour. Most tofu will have a better flavour if lightly pressed to remove excess moisture. (See Agedashi Tofu, page 192.)

17 RICE BRAN

Toasted rice bran, or nuka, is used for pickling vegetables. Similar to a sourdough starter, the bran is cultivated to create a colony of beneficial bacteria that can pickle vegetables in as little as a few hours. More on this in Nukazuke Pickles on page 18.

18 WASABI

Wasabi is the pungent relative of horseradish often served with sushi. There are a few different varieties of wasabi in Japan but the most prized is the bright green *hon-wasabi*. Traditionally it is ground on a grater made from shark skin to aerate the grated wasabi. True wasabi has a delicious flavour to match its pungency.

19 BONITO FLAKES

Bonito flakes are fine shavings of smoked, fermented and dried bonito. They are one of my favourite ingredients. You can make a stock from them in minutes, use them as a seasoning sprinkled into stir-fried dishes, or even just scatter them on top of any food to add flavour.

chapter one pickles, stocks and seasonings

Preparation is fundamental to Japanese cuisine, but it also makes excellent sense for any home cook. If you live a busy life but want to eat well, the solution will always be to cook when you can, rather than when you have to. With just a little planning and preparation, a full Japanese meal of soup and a few different dishes can be assembled in minutes, every night of the week.

This chapter is important because it shows how a cuisine fits with everyday life. It focuses on the inner workings that take an impressive and delicious dish from an ambitious project to something that is practical and realistic for you to make not once or twice, but whenever the mood takes you.

ASAZUKE PICKLES

浅漬け

ASAZUKE IS THE SIMPLEST FORM OF JAPANESE PICKLING. THIS 'SHALLOW PICKLE' TECHNIQUE
IS A USEFUL ONE TO KNOW AS IT'S THE EASIEST AND FASTEST. DON'T THINK OF IT AS PICKLING
THE VEGETABLES JUST IN SALT, AS REALLY IT'S PICKLING VEGETABLES IN THEIR OWN JUICES.

INGREDIENTS

VEGETABLES

1 carrot
1 cucumber
¼ Chinese cabbage
2 stalks celery

OTHER VEGETABLES GREAT
FOR ASAZUKE INCLUDE

Daikon
Japanese eggplant
Red radishes
Okra
Cabbage
Red cabbage

SEASONING

1 tsp salt
1 small piece kombu
    (about 5cm x 10cm),
    finely sliced (optional)

AROMATICS (optional)

½ tsp ginger juice, or
½ tsp finely sliced yuzu
    or lemon rind, or
2 shiso leaves, finely shredded

METHOD

1 Prepare the vegetables. I tend to lightly peel vegetables like
daikon and carrot, and peel cucumbers in strips if the skins are
especially tough. Most other vegetables I leave unpeeled.

2 Cut them into your preferred size and shape and place them
into a press-seal bag. How you cut the vegetables is up to you.
Asazuke may be finely shredded, or cut into larger chunks for
more individual texture.

3 Season with salt and kombu, if using, and add any aromatics
you like. Massage the bag for a minute then squeeze out as much
air as possible and seal the bag. Refrigerate for at least 30 minutes
until the vegetables are softened. You can keep these pickles in
the fridge for up to a week.

≫ If you can't find kombu, a dash of fish sauce can help to boost the
umami of the dish. It's not as strange as you think. Although we think of
fish sauce as a Southeast Asian ingredient, Japan produces quite a few
regional varieties, such as the famous Ishiru from Ishikawa prefecture.

MAKES AROUND 2 CUPS **PREPARATION TIME** 10 MINS, PLUS AT LEAST 30 MINUTES PICKLING **COOKING TIME** 0 MINS

NUKAZUKE PICKLES

糠漬け

THEY MAY TAKE A LITTLE MORE WORK, BUT THESE ARE MY
FAVOURITE PICKLES. THEY HAVE A DELICATE, MALTY AND
LACTIC SOURNESS TO THEM THAT ISN'T OVERWHELMING, BUT
SEEMS TO ENHANCE THE SWEETNESS OF THE VEGETABLES.

The role of good bacteria for our digestive systems and general
health is becoming better understood every day, and fermented
foods like these pickles play an important part in that process.

The principle behind nukazuke is one of lactic fermentation.
Living natural yeasts and lactobacilli in the roasted rice bran
pickle the vegetables and these colonies must be cultivated and
maintained. This requires regular feeding and stirring to aerate
the nuka bed (*nukadoko*). Preparing and maintaining your nuka
bed is a little like caring for a sourdough starter.

It may seem like an imposition to have to attend to your nuka
bed every day or two, but I see it as an incredible boost to
convenience. Imagine being able to simply drop a few vegetables
into your active nuka bed and then pull them out ready to eat
just a few hours later. Once you overcome any initial trepidations,
you'll see that a well-maintained nuka bed is one of the most
useful things in your kitchen.

INGREDIENTS

VEGETABLES

1 daikon
2 carrots
2 cucumbers
3 small Japanese eggplants
½ cup red radishes

NUKADOKO

800ml spring water
150g salt, plus extra for
   salting vegetables
800g roasted rice bran (*nuka*)
1 tsp mustard powder
1 tsp chilli powder

PREPARATION TIME 30 MINS, PLUS A FEW MINUTES OF MAINTENANCE DAILY **COOKING TIME** 0 MINS

METHOD

1 Bring 800ml spring water to the boil in a large saucepan and add the 150g salt, stirring to dissolve. Allow to cool to room temperature.

2 Prepare your vegetables by peeling vegetables like daikon and carrot very lightly, just remove any wiry roots or rough patches. The skin of the vegetables will improve flavour and help to maintain the bacteria in the nuka bed. Cut the vegetables into large pieces.

3 Salt the vegetables by rubbing them with a little coarse salt and allowing them to drain in a colander for a few minutes. Brush off any excess salt.

TROUBLESHOOTING

The pickles taste raw.
Raw tasting pickles means that the activity of your nuka bed is too low. This is perfectly fine, particularly in the first couple of weeks of your nuka bed. If the vegetables haven't pickled within 2 days, discard them and try inoculating the bed again with vegetable peelings.

The nuka bed smells sour.
A sour smell in the bed means that it is too acidic. Add washed eggshells or additional mustard powder to reduce the acidity and mix the nuka bed at least twice a day.

The nuka bed is too wet.
If the nuka starts to look like mud rather than damp sand, that will stop air from circulating. Blot with paper towel to remove any pooling liquid.

The vegetables are well-pickled, but lacking flavour.
You can add additional flavour to your nuka bed by incorporating umami-rich ingredients, such as strips of kombu, shiitake mushrooms or bonito flakes. Garlic is also sometimes added for a different flavour.

4 Combine the roasted rice bran, mustard and chilli powder in a dish and with clean hands, stir through the salted water a little at a time to create a crumbly paste with the consistency of damp sand. (Most brands of nuka come pre-inoculated with bacteria, which means you can skip the step of 'seeding' the bran with new bacteria. However, if you need to 'seed' your nuka bed, add some vegetable peelings to the bed and leave them for 24 hours. Then discard the peelings and stir. Repeat this process a few times.)

5 Place the vegetables into the nuka bed and 'plant' them under the surface. Lightly pat down to flatten the nuka bed on top of the vegetables. Cover the nuka bed loosely (not air tight) and leave the vegetables to pickle at room temperature. In summer the pickling process may take as little as 6 hours, but in colder weather (and in the early stages of maintaining the nuka bed) it's best to leave them for 12–24 hours.

6 Remove the vegetables from the bed. Rinse the vegetables under running water and pat dry. Slice and serve.

I'm running out of nuka.
The more you use your nuka bed the more you will need to replenish it. Prepare additional bran using the method above and combine it with your existing nuka bed. You can throw out some of the old bed to make room for the new bran. Throwing out some of the old nuka bed (rather than just adding less of the new) will reduce the risk of spoiling.

The nuka bed is mouldy.
If you see mould appearing on the surface of the bed, just scrape it off and throw it away. Stirring the bed regularly should avoid this. If mould is growing under the surface of the bed, you may need to throw it out and start again.

I'm going away and won't be able to attend to my nuka bed.
You can leave your nuka bed unattended for a few days by keeping it in the fridge and scattering the surface with a little salt to prevent mould. (You'll need to discard the surface layer when you return.) For anything longer, you'll need to either take it with you or entrust it to a friend. Otherwise, just throw it out and start a new nuka bed when you get home.

BROWN VINEGAR PICKLES

玄米酢漬け

PICKLING IN VINEGAR IS A LITTLE LESS POPULAR IN JAPAN THAN THE OTHER STYLES
OF PICKLING. VEGETABLE DISHES TEND TO BE DRESSED IN VINEGAR (SUCH AS CUCUMBER
AND WAKAME, PAGE 179) RATHER THAN PICKLED. THAT SAID, MANY LOVE THE SWEETNESS
THAT'S USED TO COUNTERBALANCE THE SHARP ACIDITY OF VINEGAR.

INGREDIENTS

VEGETABLES

1 large daikon, lightly peeled
and halved lengthways (or
quartered if very large)
2 carrots, lightly peeled and
halved lengthways
2 cucumbers, peeled in strips
and halved lengthways
3 small turnips, lightly peeled
and halved

BROWN VINEGAR PICKLING LIQUID

2 tbsp salt
4 tbsp sugar
½ cup brown rice vinegar

METHOD

1 Combine the vegetables, salt and sugar in a snug-fitting
pickling crock and stir to coat. Pour over the vinegar and screw
down the lid to hold the vegetables at the base of the crock.
Don't worry if the vegetables are not completely covered; as the
vegetables soften they will release additional liquid. Refrigerate for
at least 6 hours. If you don't have a pickling crock use an ordinary
plastic container. Place plastic wrap directly on the vegetables, and
place a weight on top.

2 To serve, slice the vegetables individually and serve a selection
on a single plate. Although they will keep for longer, these pickles
are best enjoyed within two weeks.

≫ Firm, slightly bitter vegetables like turnip and daikon
work well as vinegar pickles as the vinegar masks their
bitterness, bringing out their more complex flavours.

PREPARATION TIME 10 MINS, PLUS AT LEAST 6 HOURS PICKLING **COOKING TIME** 0 MINS

サ シ ス セ ソ

Sa	Shi	Su	Se	So
SUGAR (**sa**to)	SALT (**shi**o)	VINEGAR (**su**)	SOY SAUCE (**sho**yu)	MI**SO**

This simple mnemonic explains the principles of adding the five basic Japanese seasonings, particularly for simmered dishes. It's helpful instruction, but what's more useful to note is how it separates seasoning from flavouring.

The difference between seasoning and flavouring is an important one. In fact, it may be *the* most important thing to understand in cooking.

Seasoning is the process of balancing the taste of food on our tastebuds on our tongues, enhancing our appreciation of existing flavours. Flavouring is the process of adding aromas, to be sensed by our noses.

Our tastebuds perceive just five main tastes — sweetness, saltiness, sourness, bitterness and umami — and we season food to these tastes. The first four of these are commonly understood, and the mnemonic speaks to these. Sugar for sweetness, salt for saltiness, vinegar for sourness. Bitterness is rarely added to food as a seasoning, which leaves the umami of soy sauce and miso.

Umami is the savoury 'fifth taste' named and discovered by Japanese scientist Kikunae Ikeda in 1908, but which has been a cornerstone of Japanese cooking for thousands of years. Seasonings like soy sauce, miso, bonito flakes and kombu are all prized in Japanese cooking for their delicate savoury flavour. You'll find a source of umami in almost every Japanese dish. It could be a stock or an added sauce, or created through a process of cooking, such as seasoning meat or fish with salt and then grilling it to enhance its umami (page 122), or fermenting vegetables in rice bran (page 18).

Flavourings are the unique characteristics of our ingredients. The flavour of a carrot, the aromatic scent of *yuzu* citron, the distinct apple and earthy notes of an eggplant, the minty pepper of a shiso leaf, or the warm perfume of ginger.

We season food to bring its flavours into focus, not to overwhelm them or change them. A well-seasoned piece of fish should taste like fish, not sugar or vinegar or even miso. Choose your ingredients for their flavour, and season them to make them taste great. Japanese cooking really is that simple.

1

2

3

1 All-purpose Chicken Dashi
2 Salmon Flake
3 Boosted Soy Sauce
4 No. 1 Stock
5 Bonito Stock
6 Teriyaki Glaze

BOOSTED SOY SAUCE

うま味醤油

I USE THIS SOY SAUCE IN PLACE OF NORMAL LIGHT SOY SAUCE FOR ABSOLUTELY EVERYTHING.
IT'S LIGHTER AND LESS SALTY, BUT HAS A RICHER AND MORE BALANCED FLAVOUR.

INGREDIENTS

150ml sake
100ml mirin
1 tsp caster sugar
500ml light soy sauce
4 dried shiitake mushrooms
Handful of large bonito flakes
    (about 5g)

METHOD

1   Place the sake, mirin and sugar in a medium saucepan and
bring to a simmer. Flambé with a blowtorch, match or lighter and
allow to burn until burned out. Add the soy sauce and mushrooms
and bring back to a simmer. Add the bonito flakes and turn off
the heat. Allow the sauce to stand for 1 hour, then drain through a
muslin-lined sieve. Store the sauce in an old clean wine bottle or
soy sauce bottle in the pantry.

≫ Like most umami-rich foods, this boosted soy sauce improves with
age. I usually make a triple or quadruple batch and keep it in a big
sealed jar in the pantry. When stocks are getting a little low, I just
make a new batch and top it up. It will keep indefinitely.

MAKES ABOUT 750ML **PREPARATION TIME** 5 MINS **COOKING TIME** 10 MINS, PLUS 1 HOUR STANDING

TERIYAKI GLAZE

照り焼きのモト

IF YOU HAVE ANY OF MY OTHER BOOKS, YOU MAY HAVE SEEN THIS RECIPE BEFORE, AND FOR
GOOD REASON. THIS SIMPLE MIXTURE IS THE GREATEST SHORTCUT TO AN ENTIRE WORLD OF
JAPANESE COOKING. YOU WON'T NEED TO BUY PRE-MADE 'TERIYAKI SAUCE' EVER AGAIN.

INGREDIENTS

200ml sake
200ml mirin
250ml soy sauce
60g caster sugar

METHOD

1   Combine all the ingredients in a small saucepan and stir
over medium heat until the sugar dissolves completely. Transfer
to a bottle (I use an old soy sauce bottle) and store in the pantry.

≫ This will keep in the pantry indefinitely, but I guarantee you'll use
it all and be making your next batch before you know it.

MAKES ABOUT 650ML **PREPARATION TIME** 2 MINS **COOKING TIME** 3 MINS

SALMON FLAKE

鮭フレーク

SALMON FLAKE IS A POPULAR INGREDIENT IN MODERN JAPANESE HOME COOKING,
USED IN ONIGIRI, PASTA, SANDWICHES, SALADS OR EVEN JUST SCATTERED OVER
HOT RICE FOR A SUPER-FAST MEAL. IT'S EASY TO MAKE YOUR OWN.

INGREDIENTS

2 whole salmon carcasses,
   or 500g salmon fillets
½ tsp salt

METHOD

1 Heat your oven to 150°C. Place the carcasses or fillets on a
baking tray and bake for about 20 minutes until cooked through.
Using your fingers, carefully pick all the meat from the bones,
discarding any bones, skin and cartilage. If using whole carcasses,
don't forget the meat in the head, particularly around the cheek area.

2 Place the meat into a mortar and pound with a pestle to break
it into a coarse paste. You may need to do this in batches.

3 Place the fish paste in a dry frying pan over low–medium heat
and season with salt. Fry for about 20 minutes, stirring to break
up any clumps, then remove from the heat and allow to cool. The
salmon should feel quite dry. Rub the salmon between your
fingers to create very fine flakes.

4 Return the salmon to the frying pan for a further 20 minutes,
stirring occasionally until you have dry flakes. Heat your oven to
60°C and place the pan in the oven for an hour to allow the flakes
to dry completely.

5 Remove from the oven, allow the flakes to cool to room
temperature and transfer to an airtight container. This will store
well in the fridge or at room temperature, but I prefer to store it in
the freezer as it will keep longer and you can use it straight from
the freezer without thawing.

≫ Salmon carcasses are available from fishmongers. They take a little
more work to pick clean than fillets do but they're a fraction of the price.

MAKES ABOUT 1–2 CUPS **PREPARATION TIME** 30 MINS **COOKING TIME** 2 HOURS

NO. 1 STOCK

一番出汁

ICHIBAN DASHI IS THE CENTREPIECE OF JAPANESE CUISINE, IN THE SAME WAY THAT CHICKEN STOCK IS AT THE HEART OF FRENCH CUISINE. THE BIG DIFFERENCE IS THAT IT TAKES JUST MINUTES TO MAKE SO THERE'S NO EXCUSE NOT TO HAVE DASHI TO HAND.

INGREDIENTS

1 piece dried kombu
(approximately 10cm square)
1½ litres cold water
15g bonito flakes

≫ Kombu can be hard to come by, so if you can't find it I suggest just using Bonito Stock (page 30) or All-purpose Chicken Dashi (page 31) instead.

METHOD

1 Wipe the kombu with a dry cloth to remove any dirt. Put the kombu and cold water into a saucepan and place over medium heat. Bring the water to a simmer and simmer the kombu until it is softened enough so that your fingernail leaves a mark in the kombu when you press it (this will be well before the water starts to boil). Remove the kombu and discard.

2 Increase the heat and bring the liquid in the saucepan to the boil. Add the bonito flakes, count 2 seconds then turn off the heat. Allow the bonito flakes to stand for about 10 minutes until they sink to the bottom, skimming off any frothy scum that comes to the surface of the liquid. Don't stir. Strain the stock through a muslin-lined sieve. Cool to room temperature then keep in the fridge for up to a week.

MAKES 1½ LITRES **PREPARATION TIME** 0 MINS **COOKING TIME** 10 MINS

BONITO STOCK

鰹出汁

THIS STOCK IS MADE BY SIMPLY INFUSING WATER WITH THE TASTE OF DRIED BONITO FLAKES.

INGREDIENTS

750ml water
20g bonito flakes

≫ Alternatively, instead of straining, you can wrap the bonito flakes in a small piece of muslin and tie into a parcel before adding to the boiling water.

METHOD

1 Bring the water to a rolling boil in a small saucepan. Add the bonito flakes and boil for 2 seconds. Turn off the heat and allow the bonito flakes to sink to the bottom of the pot without stirring. Carefully skim any scum from the surface of the stock then strain the stock through a muslin-lined sieve. Cool to room temperature then keep in the fridge for up to a week.

MAKES 750ML **PREPARATION TIME** 2 MINS **COOKING TIME** 10 MINS

ALL-PURPOSE CHICKEN DASHI

万能鶏出汁

THIS IS NOT A TRADITIONAL JAPANESE STOCK BUT IT'S THE ONE I MAKE MOST OFTEN. THE STRONG, RICH FLAVOUR AND TEXTURE OF THIS STOCK IS HARD TO BEAT. I USE IT FOR JUST ABOUT ANYTHING, FROM SOUPS AND RISOTTOS, TO STIR-FRIES AND BEEF STEWS.

INGREDIENTS

500g chicken bones
About 3 litres water
20g bonito flakes

METHOD

1   Place the chicken bones in a medium saucepan and cover with an ample amount of cold water. Bring to the boil and boil for about a minute until a raft of scum forms, then remove from the heat. Discard the water and rinse both the pot and bones to remove all traces of scum.

2   Return the bones to the pot and cover with cold water. Bring to a very low simmer (bubbles breaking the surface only occasionally) and simmer partially covered for about 4 hours. After 4 hours, add the bonito flakes to the stock and remove from the heat.

3   Allow to stand for 15 minutes, then strain through muslin or a very fine sieve. Cool to room temperature then keep in the fridge for up to a week.

≫ The long simmering process should lightly brown the bones as the water level reduces, giving the stock a light golden colour.

MAKES ABOUT 2 LITRES   **PREPARATION TIME** 2 MINS   **COOKING TIME** 4½ HOURS

chapter japanese
two breakfasts

Fish for breakfast? For lovers of Japanese food, the Japanese breakfast may be the meal that holds the most fascination. It can be a selection of dishes that might look impossibly elaborate next to a bowl of cereal or bacon and eggs with toast.

Japanese breakfasts are rarely served in restaurants outside Japan, although anyone staying at a fancy hotel anywhere in the world might question the wisdom of including pickles and soup in the breakfast buffet until they see the smiles on the faces of an appreciative Japanese family far from home.

The additional complication is that there are very few specific breakfast foods in Japanese cuisine — that is to say, foods that are only eaten at breakfast. Any of the dishes in this chapter could easily be served at lunch or dinner — and they often are — but when placed on a breakfast table they make complete sense.

HOT-SPRING EGGS

温泉卵

THESE SOFT-COOKED EGGS ARE EVERYWHERE IN JAPAN. THEY'RE USED TO TOP RICE DISHES, NOODLES, PASTA OR JUST EATEN ON THEIR OWN. TRADITIONALLY MADE BY HOLDING A BASKET OF EGGS IN THERMAL HOT SPRINGS, HERE'S HOW TO MAKE THEM AT HOME.

INGREDIENTS

4 fresh free-range eggs
1 tsp finely chopped chives,
   to serve (optional)

EGG TARE (Optional)
½ cup Bonito Stock (page 30)
1 tbsp mirin
1 tbsp soy sauce

METHOD

1 SLOW METHOD Heat a large saucepan of water to exactly 63°C using a thermometer to accurately check the temperature. Add the eggs and return the water to that temperature. Cook the eggs for 45 minutes, adjusting the heat as required to maintain the precise temperature over the cooking period. If you have a steam oven with a sous vide setting, just set it to 63°C and place the eggs on a tray inside for 45 minutes.

FAST METHOD Place 1 litre water in a medium-sized heavy saucepan with a tight-fitting lid (a cast-iron casserole dish would be perfect). Bring to the boil then turn off the heat and add 1 cup of room temperature water. Add the eggs and cover the pan. Allow to stand for 12 minutes, then uncover and remove the eggs.

2 For the egg tare, bring the stock and mirin to the boil in a small saucepan and boil for a minute until halved in volume. Remove from the heat, add the soy sauce and allow to cool to room temperature.

3 To serve, crack the cooked eggs into separate small bowls as you would a normal raw egg. Dress with the egg tare and sprinkle with the chopped chives if using.

≫ These eggs have caused me an awful lot of frustration over the years, so be warned. The slow method will produce great results every time, but if you want to try the fast method a lot will depend on your saucepan, size of eggs, temperature of eggs and amount of water. A bit of trial and error may be needed until you find your own perfect formula.

SERVES 4 **PREPARATION TIME** 5 MINS **COOKING TIME** SLOW METHOD: 45 MINS; FAST METHOD: 12 MINS

BACON AND SPINACH STIR-FRY

ベーコンとほうれん草の炒めもの

THIS SIMPLE TWO-INGREDIENT STIR-FRY IS OFTEN EATEN WITH RICE AND A FRIED EGG
FOR BREAKFAST, BUT IT'S ALSO GREAT ON TOAST OR AS A BASE FOR EGGS BENEDICT.

INGREDIENTS

100g thick-cut bacon, cut into
    batons
1 tbsp butter
1 bunch spinach (2–3 plants),
    washed, trimmed and cut
    into 5cm lengths
¼ tsp salt
2 tsp sake
Freshly ground pepper

METHOD

1 Add the bacon to a cold frying pan and place it over high heat. As the fat renders from the bacon, toss the bacon to fry until browned all over. If your bacon is particularly lean, you may need to add a little oil.

2 Add the butter, spinach, salt and sake, and toss until the spinach is wilted. Grind over a little pepper and serve.

≫ You don't have to break out a wok every time you want to stir-fry something. Many Japanese-style stir-fried dishes are made in an ordinary frying pan.

SERVES 2 **PREPARATION TIME** 5 MINS **COOKING TIME** 5 MINS

GRANDMA'S RICE PORRIDGE

おばあちゃんのお粥

RICE PORRIDGE IS THE KIND OF DISH YOU HAVE A RELATIONSHIP WITH. IT'S WHAT YOUR
PARENTS OR GRANDPARENTS MAKE FOR YOU WHEN YOU'RE SICK AND EVERY MOUTHFUL IS
A REMINDER OF HOW MUCH THEY CARE FOR YOU. THIS THICK AND HEARTY VERSION IS THE
PORRIDGE ASAMI'S LATE GRANDMOTHER USED TO MAKE FOR HER WHEN SHE WAS A CHILD.

INGREDIENTS

1 cup cooked rice (see method
on page 52)
3 cups All-purpose Chicken
Dashi (page 31), or other
stock
¼ tsp salt
2 tsp white or brown miso
2 eggs, beaten
¼ sheet nori, cut into batons
2 thin spring onions, finely
sliced
Pickles such as *umeboshi*
(salted plums), to serve
(optional)

METHOD

1 Place the cooked rice, stock and salt in a medium saucepan
and bring to a simmer. Simmer, covered, for 30 minutes or until
the porridge reaches the consistency you like, then stir through
the miso.

2 Stir through the beaten egg until just set, then remove from
the heat and top with the nori and spring onions. Serve with the
pickles.

≫ Try not to boil the egg in the porridge, particularly if it's thin, as the
egg proteins can cause a thin porridge to separate in the same way
an egg raft clarifies a French consommé.

SERVES 4 **PREPARATION TIME** 10 MINS **COOKING TIME** 45 MINS

一汁三菜

Ichijyuu sansai

A soup and three dishes.

Ichijyuu sansai is the model of a complete Japanese meal, consisting of a soup and three dishes plus a bowl of rice and a plate of pickles, elements so ubiquitous and necessary they need not even be mentioned. Breakfast, lunch or dinner, the format of the meal remains the same.

At the ideological centre of a meal, a bowl of rice is not considered an accompaniment or side dish, but rather the axle on which the rest of the meal turns (see Chapter 3). Along with the rice comes a simple plate of pickles (see Chapter 1), adding balance both in flavour and temperature to the warm soup and other dishes. Variations of miso soup are the most popular served with this kind of complete meal, but it could equally be any variety of clear soup (see Chapter 4) if you preferred. The three *sansai* dishes often take the form of one main dish – perhaps a piece of grilled fish (see Chapter 6), or a braised meaty dish (see Chapter 7) – and two secondary dishes, smaller offerings consisting mainly of vegetables (see Chapter 8).

You'll find *ichijyuu sansai* meals everywhere in Japan: served on an individual tray for breakfast at an exclusive *ryokan*, gathered one dish at a time in an office cafeteria, packed together into a convenience store bento, or lovingly placed in the centre of a family dinner table. Regardless of how it's served, it is always eaten by grazing across the dishes – a bite of fish here, followed by a mouthful of vegetables, a sip of soup and over to the rice, then maybe some pickles to cleanse the palate before heading back for another sip of soup. It may sound a little confusing but it's actually very intuitive.

When assembling an *ichijyuu sansai* menu, consider the overall balance of the meal. An oily main dish may be offset with fresher secondary dishes. A lighter main may be anchored by a similarly weighted soup, rather than being overpowered by something more robust. You'll be surprised how satisfying a balanced meal like this can be.

There are, of course, other ways of eating Japanese food, multi-course formal *cha-kaiseki* menus, simple one-bowl individual *donburi*, even *ichijyuu issai*, an austere offering of just one soup and one dish, but the *ichijyuu sansai* model is one of ordinary completeness, neither wanting nor indulgent. The classic Japanese breakfast shown on the next page is a perfect example.

FULL JAPANESE BREAKFAST

和風朝ごはん

THIS MAY NOT BE THE KIND OF BREAKFAST I THROW TOGETHER ON A TUESDAY MORNING
TRYING TO GET THE KIDS FED AND CHANGED AND OUT THE DOOR BEFORE PEAK HOUR, BUT
IT'S REALLY NO MORE EFFORT THAN A FULL ENGLISH OF BACON, SAUSAGES, EGGS, MUSHROOMS
AND TOAST. IT'S ONLY THE ROLLED OMELETTE (*TAMAGOYAKI*) THAT TAKES SOME DOING, BUT IF
GOING TO THIS LEVEL OF EFFORT FOR BREAKFAST IS MORE THAN YOU'RE WILLING TO BEAR,
TRY THE DASHI EGGS ON RICE (PAGE 47) FOR A QUICK AND EASY VERSION.

INGREDIENTS

1 salmon fillet (about 200g),
   skin-on but scaled
1 serve Miso Soup of your
   choice (pages 80–83)
1 serve Pickles of your choice
   (pages 16–23)
1 serve Quick Soy-steeped
   Spinach (page 174)
2 cups Wholegrain Rice
   (page 52)

TAMAGOYAKI

4 eggs
4 tbsp Bonito Stock (page 30)
2 tsp caster sugar
1 tsp soy sauce
1 tbsp vegetable oil
½ cup grated daikon, to serve

METHOD

1   For the *tamagoyaki*, beat the eggs, stock, sugar and soy sauce
together, and transfer to a jug. Dip a piece of paper towel into the
oil and brush a medium frying pan with the oil. Heat the pan over
medium heat, pour half the egg into the pan and fry until just set,
pushing the eggs around to create folds. Using chopsticks, gently
flip the egg from one edge, creating a roll from one side of the pan
to the other (like rolling up a carpet). Brush the pan with more
oil and slide the roll of egg back to the handle end. Add half the
remaining egg to the open side of the pan and roll the egg roll back
to the far edge to create a thicker roll. Repeat the process with the
remaining egg. Remove the roll from the pan and mould into a bar
shape using a bamboo mat or tea towel and allow to cool. Slice into
thick slices and top with the grated daikon, stained with a dash of
soy sauce.

2   Halve the salmon lengthways to create two thick fillets. Grill or
fry the fillets as for Shioyaki (page 122). Serve with the *tamagoyaki*,
miso soup, pickles, spinach and rice.

≫ A Japanese rolled omelette is normally made in a specifically designed
square or rectangular pan called a *makiyakinabe* (rolling frying pan). You
can buy non-stick versions relatively cheaply at Japanese grocers, or just
use an ordinary round frying pan. Making this omelette isn't easy, and
can take quite a bit of practice.

SERVES 2 **PREPARATION TIME** 20 MINS **COOKING TIME** 30 MINS

BROWN BUTTER, SALMON FLAKE AND SHIITAKE TOAST

鮭と椎茸のパン

THIS IS A BIT LIKE A JAPANESE VERSION OF EGGS AND TOAST SOLDIERS.
IT'S NOT AT ALL A TRADITIONAL JAPANESE DISH, BUT IT IS DELICIOUS.

INGREDIENTS

50g unsalted butter
4 slices good quality wholemeal
  bread
1 tsp salt flakes
4 tbsp Salmon Flake (page 29)
2 tbsp finely chopped chives
2 dried shiitake mushrooms
4 Hot-spring Eggs, to serve
  (page 34)

METHOD

1 For the brown butter, melt the butter in a small saucepan over medium heat, swirling occasionally, for about 5 minutes until the butter is light caramel brown with a nutty aroma.

2 Toast the bread and spoon the butter over the toast, season with salt flakes and scatter with Salmon Flake and chives. Using a rasp grater, grate the shiitake generously over the top. Serve with the Hot-spring Eggs.

≫ I use grated dried shiitake mushrooms on pasta, risotto, roast chicken and many other dishes. They're a cheap substitute for dried porcini.

SERVES 4 **PREPARATION TIME** 15 MINS **COOKING TIME** 10 MINS

DASHI EGGS ON RICE

だし焼き卵のご飯かけ

WHEN WE DON'T HAVE TIME (OR THE ENERGY) TO MAKE A FULL JAPANESE BREAKFAST, THIS SIMPLIFIED ONE-BOWL VERSION IS A PERFECT SOLUTION. OUR FAMILY LOVES THIS RECIPE, AND IT'S ONE OF OUR MOST COMMONLY EATEN DISHES.

INGREDIENTS

1½ cups cooked rice, hot
2 tbsp Salmon Flake (page 29)
2 tsp aonori (green dried nori seaweed flakes) or finely chopped chives

DASHI EGGS

3 large eggs
¼ cup All-purpose Chicken Dashi (page 31), or other stock
1 tsp caster sugar
¼ tsp salt
1½ tbsp vegetable oil

METHOD

1 Mix the eggs, stock, sugar and salt in a large bowl until well-combined but try not to incorporate too much air into the mixture. Place the cooked rice into two serving bowls (do this before you start frying the eggs).

2 Heat a medium frying pan over medium heat and add the oil, then rotate the pan to ensure it is completely coated. Pour the eggs into the frying pan and allow to stand for just a few seconds. Draw a spatula through the eggs three or four times in long slow strokes, as if making an omelette. While the eggs are still quite runny, divide into half and transfer straight over the rice. Scatter with the Salmon Flake and aonori flakes and serve immediately.

≫ Just like scrambled eggs, the dashi eggs should be very runny when you take them out of the pan. They will keep firming long after they're off the heat.

SERVES 2 **PREPARATION TIME** 5 MINS **COOKING TIME** 3 MINS

WHOLEMEAL HOTCAKES

全粒粉のホットケーキ

A SHORT STACK OF THICK AMERICAN-STYLE HOTCAKES IS A POPULAR DISH IN JAPAN
FOR BREAKFAST OR AFTERNOON TEA. WE LOVE THIS WHOLEMEAL VERSION.

INGREDIENTS

300g (2 cups) plain wholemeal
  flour
2 tbsp baking powder
2 eggs
2 tbsp caster sugar
360g (1½ cups) natural
  yoghurt
½ cup milk
50g butter, to serve
½ cup maple syrup, to serve

METHOD

1 Sift the flour and baking powder into a large mixing bowl to
remove any clumps. Tip any bran remaining in the sieve into the
bowl as well. Crack the eggs into a separate bowl, add the sugar
and whisk until the sugar is dissolved. Add the yoghurt and milk
and whisk until smooth.

2 Make a well in the centre of the flour and add the yoghurt
mixture. Slowly whisk the liquids and solids together until just
combined. A few lumps is fine. Rest the batter in the fridge for
at least 15 minutes or until ready to use.

3 Heat a non-stick frying pan over medium heat and ladle in
the batter, teasing it into a circle. You don't need to grease the
pan if it is non-stick. Fry the hotcake until nicely browned (about
90 seconds), then flip it and cook the other side until the hotcake
is cooked through. You can tell when it is cooked by pressing
on the centre of the hotcake. When it springs back, the batter
is cooked. Repeat for the remaining batter. I use two pans to
make two hotcakes simultaneously, as they need to be served
immediately for best results.

4 Place two hotcakes in a stack and top with a little pat of chilled
butter. Pour over the maple syrup and serve.

≫ It may seem strange to pour the bran back into the flour but the
point of sifting is just to remove clumps. The bran adds a lovely texture
to the hotcakes as well as extra fibre.

SERVES 3–4 **PREPARATION TIME** 15 MINS **COOKING TIME** 15 MINS

chapter rice and three noodles

It would be hard to overstate the importance of rice to Japanese cuisine. A simple bowl of steamed rice forms the centre of nearly every Japanese meal, but it's also drunk alongside as *nihonshu* (what we would call 'sake'), and incorporated in the production of many of the most common seasonings, from vinegar to cooking wines to soy sauce. Glutinous rice is pounded into flour and used for sweets, and rice bran is even used as a bed for pickling vegetables. It's safe to say that rice is the bedrock of Japanese food.

If a Japanese meal doesn't include rice, then odds are you're eating noodles. Ramen, udon and soba are icons of the cuisine, and it's worth getting to know them.

WHOLEGRAIN RICE

十二穀米

IN RECENT YEARS JAPAN HAS SEEN A BOOM IN RICE MIXES LIKE THESE, WHERE A RANGE OF WHOLE GRAINS ARE ADDED TO ORDINARY WHITE RICE FOR FLAVOUR AND TO BOOST ITS FIBRE CONTENT. MAKE A BATCH OF THE RICE MIX AND KEEP IT IN THE PANTRY, ADDING A FEW SCOOPS TO EVERY BATCH OF RICE YOU COOK. WE RARELY EAT PLAIN WHITE RICE ANYMORE. THIS IS JUST TOO DELICIOUS.

INGREDIENTS

3 cups short-grain white koshihikari rice (sold in Australia as 'sushi rice') or 2 cups short-grain koshihikari rice and 1 cup brown rice
2 tbsp Wholegrain Rice Mix
4 tbsp water, extra

WHOLEGRAIN RICE MIX

¼ cup millet
¼ cup amaranth
1 tbsp red quinoa
¼ cup rolled barley
2 tsp buckwheat
¼ cup pearl glutinous rice
2 tbsp sorghum
2 tbsp roasted black beans
2 tbsp dried azuki beans
¼ cup black rice
1 tbsp Thai red rice
2 tsp toasted sesame seeds
1 tsp toasted black sesame seeds

METHOD

1 For the Wholegrain Rice Mix, combine all the ingredients in an airtight container and keep in a cool, dry place to use as needed.

2 To cook the rice, it is best to use a rice cooker. Wash the rice well under running water and cover with the appropriate amount of water according to the rice cooker instructions. Add the Wholegrain Rice Mix and stir it through the rice. Cook as normal.

To cook the rice on a stove, use a heavy saucepan with a heavy lid. Wash the short-grain rice well under running water and cover with cold water to 2 cm above the level of the rice. Add the Wholegrain Rice Mix, stir it through the rice and allow to stand for at least 2 hours (but you can even soak the rice and mixture overnight if you prefer). Bring the pot to a boil over high heat, uncovered, until the water level reaches the top of the rice and you can see bubbles of steam escaping from the surface of the rice. Cover the pot with the heavy lid and reduce the heat to very low. Continue to cook for 12 minutes, then turn off the heat.

3 When the rice cooker or stovetop cooking method has finished, allow the rice to stand for a further 5 minutes without removing the lid. Fluff the rice with a cutting motion using a rice paddle and allow to dry with the lid open for 3 minutes. Close the lid and keep warm until ready to serve.

≫ A pressurised rice cooker will help the grains to soften, so you don't need to let this mixture soak; however, every rice cooker is different. If you find some of the tougher grains a bit hard, soak the grains and rice together before cooking. Anything from two hours through to overnight soaking will help to soften the texture of the grains and improve the overall texture of the rice.

MAKES ABOUT 2 CUPS WHOLEGRAIN RICE MIX **PREPARATION TIME** 10 MINS **COOKING TIME** 30 MINS, PLUS SOAKING TIME

SALMON FLAKE RICE BALLS

鮭のおにぎり

SUSHI MIGHT BE THE MOST WELL-KNOWN JAPANESE RICE DISH, BUT ONIGIRI ARE WHAT
JAPANESE PEOPLE EAT EVERY DAY, FROM SNACKS TO PACKED LUNCHES. THEY CAN BE
FLAVOURED WITH JUST ABOUT ANYTHING.

INGREDIENTS

3 tbsp Salmon Flake (page 29)
3 tsp aonori (green dried nori
  seaweed flakes)
2 tsp toasted sesame seeds
3 cups cooked short-grain rice,
  warm

METHOD

1 Mix the Salmon Flake, aonori and sesame seeds through the
warm rice and divide the rice into four equal portions (¾ cup
cooked rice in each). Wet your hands and mould the rice into a
triangular puck, flattened on the sides. The rice should be pressed
so that it just holds together without being mashed.

2 Serve immediately, or wrap in aluminium foil or plastic wrap
to eat later but keep at room temperature.

≫ Never refrigerate rice balls. They're best when freshly made and
slightly warm or at room temperature if you're packing them to eat
later. Refrigeration will make the rice dry and chalky.

SERVES 2–4 **PREPARATION TIME** 5 MINS **COOKING TIME** 0 MINS

SUSHI SANDWICHES

おにぎらず

THESE SIMPLE SUSHI SANDWICHES HAVE BECOME PHENOMENALLY POPULAR IN JAPAN OVER THE LAST FEW YEARS, PARTICULARLY FOR PACKED LUNCHES. KNOWN IN JAPAN AS *ONIGIRAZU*, THEY'RE VERY SIMPLE TO MAKE, THEY DON'T NEED VINEGARED SUSHI RICE (ALTHOUGH YOU CAN USE IT IF YOU LIKE), AND THEY'RE JUST AS AT HOME WITH WESTERN SANDWICH FILLINGS AS THEY ARE WITH SUSHI-STYLE FILLINGS. GIVE THEM A TRY.

INGREDIENTS

1 cup cooked rice per sandwich
1 sheet nori per sandwich
Your favourite sandwich
   or sushi fillings (some
   suggestions below)

METHOD

1   Place a sheet of nori on a piece of plastic wrap on a cutting board with the shiny side facing down. Spread ½ cup rice in a 10cm square at 45° to the nori. Top the rice square with your choice of filling and cover with the remaining ½ cup rice.

2   Fold the corners of the nori sheet into the centre to create a square with the filling inside. Gather the plastic wrap around the sandwich and leave wrapped for at least 10 minutes for the seaweed to soften and stick to the rice. This will help hold the sandwich together. Use a sharp knife moistened with a little cold water to slice through the centre of the sandwich to reveal the filling, and serve.

SOME FILLINGS WE LIKE INCLUDE
‣ Prawn and avocado
‣ Ham, cheese and tomato
‣ Teriyaki chicken and green beans
‣ Salmon, salmon roe, egg and lettuce.

≫ Just like the rice balls, don't keep these sandwiches in the fridge. Eat them straight away or pack them in plastic wrap or foil at room temperature to eat later.

SERVES 1, BUT MAKE AS MANY AS YOU LIKE   **PREPARATION TIME** 10 MINS   **COOKING TIME** 0 MINS

魚は殿様に
もちは乞食に
焼かせろ

Sakana ha tonosama ni mochi ha kojiki ni yakasero

Let a lord grill fish and a beggar grill rice cakes.

This is an ancient instruction on how to cook. A lazy lord will grill fish without much effort, turning it only a few times, but a hungry beggar will grill impatiently, turning the rice cakes again and again to try to rush the process.

Luckily, the lord's laziness will work to his advantage, as by letting the delicate fish grill at its own pace it will be more moist and less likely to break apart. The beggar, too, for all his impatience will produce a nicely dried and evenly toasted rice cake.

We could learn a lot from the lord when it comes to cooking. Too often we prod and poke at our food while it's cooking despite the fact that for the most part these attentions will do nothing to aid the cooking and will in fact often be to its detriment. It's an instinct born from a lack of confidence. We're desperate to know if we're burning something, overcooking it, or spoiling it in some other way. Or perhaps we're just too curious? Who doesn't know the feeling of desperately wanting to open an oven door to check on the progress of a cake, knowing full well that it will do more harm than good?

Cooking – as well as many other pursuits in life – will benefit from a bit of confidence. Trust your experience and your instinct. Things may go wrong once in a while but that is the best way to learn. Problems in any kitchen are well in the past by the time the next meal comes along.

Cook more often, cook better, cook proudly, and to hell with any mistakes.

SALMON OCHAZUKE

鮭のお茶漬け

POURING TEA OVER A BOWL OF RICE AND SALMON MIGHT SEEM WEIRD,
BUT THE RESULT IS WARM, DELICIOUS, SAVOURY AND FULL OF TEXTURE.

INGREDIENTS

150g salmon fillet
½ tsp salt
1 tsp vegetable oil
2 cups hot water
2 tbsp sencha or houjicha
   tea leaves

TO SERVE

2 cups warm, cooked short-
   grain rice
Few pinches of salt
Few sprigs of mitsuba or
   watercress, cut into
   2cm lengths
½ tsp toasted sesame seeds
2 tbsp okaki rice crackers
½ sheet nori, very finely sliced
Wasabi, to serve (optional)

METHOD

1 Season the salmon fillet with salt. Heat the vegetable oil in a small frying pan over medium heat and fry the fillet for about 3–4 minutes on each side until cooked through and slightly on the dry side. Drain on paper towel and when cooled, break apart with chopsticks.

2 Heat 2 cups of hot water to 80°C and add to the tea leaves in a teapot. Allow to steep for 3 minutes.

3 Place the rice into a bowl and season with a little salt. Top with the mitsuba or watercress and flaked salmon. Scatter with the sesame seeds and rice crackers. Place the nori and a small amount of wasabi, if using, on top. Serve with the tea separate. Pour the tea over the rice and eat.

≫ Be careful if you're planning to serve this when people come to visit. In Japan, offering ochazuke is considered a signal to a guest that they have overstayed their welcome.

SERVES 2 **PREPARATION TIME** 15 MINS **COOKING TIME** 15 MINS

SUMMER RAMEN

冷やし中華

RAMEN IS ONE OF JAPAN'S FAVOURITE FOODS, BUT IN THE HUMID JAPANESE SUMMERS PEOPLE
DON'T OFTEN FEEL LIKE A BIG BOWL OF HOT SOUP. EVERY *RAMEN-YA* IN THE COUNTRY WILL HAVE
A CHILLED VERSION WITHOUT SOUP ON THE MENU IN THE HOTTER MONTHS. IT'S REALLY EASY
TO MAKE AND IT'S ON OUR TABLE WEEKLY AT THE HEIGHT OF SUMMER.

INGREDIENTS

1 chicken breast fillet
1 tsp salt
1 tsp vegetable oil
2 eggs, beaten
600g fresh thin egg noodles
150g leg ham, cut into very
    fine matchsticks
3 thick spring onions, cut into
    very fine matchsticks
1 tomato, cut into wedges
1 Lebanese cucumber, cut into
    very fine matchsticks
1 small carrot, peeled and cut
    into very fine matchsticks
2 tbsp red pickled ginger
    (*benishouga*)
½ cup Wa-fu Dressing
    (page 104) or Sesame
    Dressing (page 103)

METHOD

1 For the chicken breast, bring a small saucepan of water to a
very low simmer. Steam should rise from the water with just a few
bubbles forming at the base of the pan. Add the whole fillet and
continue to heat for just 2 minutes then cover tightly and remove
from the heat. Stand, covered, for a further 10 minutes. Remove
the chicken breast, rub a little salt on your hands and finely
shred the meat.

2 Heat a frying pan over medium heat and add the vegetable oil.
Season the beaten eggs with a little salt and pour into the pan,
rotating the pan to create a thin layer of egg. Cook for about
2 minutes until the egg is cooked through, then remove to a cutting
board. Allow to cool, then roll the egg and slice into very thin strips.

3 Bring a large pot of unsalted water to the boil and cook the
noodles according to the packet directions. Drain then rinse well
under cold running water until the noodles are cool to the touch.
Drain well.

4 Place the noodles on a serving plate, add piles of the chicken,
ham, spring onions, tomato, cucumber, carrot and pickled ginger.
Pour over the dressing to serve.

≫ Cut the vegetables really finely – ideally at least as thin as the noodles.
Vegetables cut too thickly will ruin the texture of the dish.

SERVES 4 **PREPARATION TIME** 25 MINS **COOKING TIME** 20 MINS

TUNA TARTARE DONBURI

ネギトロ丼

A 'DONBURI' IS A ONE-BOWL DISH OF RICE WITH VARIOUS TOPPINGS THAT STARTED
OUT AS A CHEAP WORKERS' LUNCH AROUND TOKYO. THE TOPPINGS CAN BE AS ELABORATE
AS A SELECTION OF SEAFOOD, A FRIED CUTLET, OR STEWED MEATS, OR THEY CAN BE AS
SIMPLE AS A BIT OF CHOPPED TUNA AND SPRING ONION.

INGREDIENTS

200g sashimi-grade tuna
2 cups cooked white rice
½ sheet nori, very thinly sliced
4 shiso leaves
4–6 thin spring onions, finely
   sliced
½ tsp wasabi, to serve
1 tbsp pickled ginger, to serve
1 tbsp Boosted Soy Sauce
   (page 28)

METHOD

1 Roughly chop the tuna into a very coarse mince.

2 Divide the rice between two bowls. Scatter the rice with the nori and lay two leaves of shiso in each bowl. Top the shiso with minced tuna and scatter everything with the sliced spring onions.

3 Serve with a small amount of wasabi and pickled ginger and the soy sauce on the side.

≫ While the main topping of a donburi takes centre stage, the various bit players of the ensemble can often steal the show. Pickled ginger, a touch of wasabi, the crunch of nori, and the aroma of shiso all work together to round out the dish, and it would not be the same without them.

SERVES 2 **PREPARATION TIME** 10 MINS **COOKING TIME** 0 MINS

酒は百薬の長

Sake ha hyaku yaku no chou

Sake has the power of 100 medicines.

No discussion of Japanese cuisine would be complete without mentioning sake. Taken at face value, this proverb might be seen as giving the green light for anyone to head out and hit the bottle in the name of good health, but happily that's not the case. There are just as many proverbs in Japanese culture decrying those who habitually drink to excess.

The understanding here is that a drink now and then can be a very beneficial thing, and it was a conclusion reached long before modern science drew the connection between moderate alcohol consumption, lowered cholesterol, and reduced rates of diseases including diabetes and heart disease.

What sets Japanese sake apart from other drinks is that it's specifically made to be paired with food. Drinking in Japanese culture rarely takes place without food present.

Sake is made by polishing rice to remove its bran and outer layers. Rice has more proteins and minerals in the outer layers of each grain than in the starchier centres. The degree of polishing has a large impact on the flavour of the resulting sake and the more polished grades of sake, such as *ginjo* (polished until less than 60 per cent of the original rice remains) and *daiginjo* (less than 50 per cent remains), tend to be held in high regard. The polished rice is then steamed, inoculated with koji mould, fermented and brewed, much like a beer or wine might be, and then usually filtered and bottled. Some sakes may also have distilled alcohol added to develop flavour. Those that do not have alcohol added are referred to as *junmai*.

Like wine, matching sake with food can be as simple or as complex as your level of interest. As a general rule, the more refined sakes like *ginjo* and *daiginjo* varieties with a higher rate of polishing the rice will have a lighter, cleaner flavour than those with lower rates of polishing, and are therefore more appropriately matched to lighter and more delicate dishes. *Honjozo* varieties (less than 70 per cent of the rice remains) may be slightly more savoury and acidic, although the addition of alcohol helps to temper those characteristics. Ordinary *junmai* sake from less polished rice will tend to be the most robust in terms of their umami savouriness and acidity, and are therefore suited to more strongly flavoured dishes.

Sake may be served at many different temperatures, ranging from highly chilled to piping hot, and this will also have a pronounced effect on flavour. Taste a refined sake chilled and then let it warm to room temperature and taste again to experience this for yourself, as it is a useful tool to employ when matching sake across a number of dishes.

This is, of course, an overly simplistic introduction to the world of sake, and you may choose to follow your curiosity with further study at your own peril. The study of sake can be fascinating and consuming, but there is no better drink to pair with Japanese cuisine.

HAND-ROLLED FAMILY SUSHI

手巻き寿司

MOST OF THE TIME THE SUSHI WE SEE ARE DELICATELY MOULDED NIGIRI SUSHI OR NEATLY ROLLED THICK ROLLS WE MIGHT GRAB FOR AN OFFICE LUNCH. JAPANESE FAMILIES AT HOME HARDLY EVER MAKE THESE, PREFERRING INSTEAD THIS SIMPLE HAND-ROLLED SUSHI. JUST LAY ALL YOUR INGREDIENTS OUT IN THE CENTRE OF THE TABLE AND LET EVERYONE MAKE THEIR OWN.

INGREDIENTS

VARIOUS SLICED SUSHI FILLINGS SUCH AS

Sashimi (sliced raw fish)
Cucumber
Avocado
Tamagoyaki (see page 43)
Salmon roe
Snow pea sprouts
Shiso leaves
Nori, to serve
Wasabi, to serve
Pickled ginger, to serve
Boosted Soy Sauce (page 28), to serve

SUSHI RICE

4 cups short-grain rice
125ml rice wine vinegar
30g caster sugar
5g salt

METHOD

1   For the sushi rice, cook the rice according to the Wholegrain Rice method on page 52, but don't add the wholegrain rice mix.

2   Place the vinegar, caster sugar and salt in a saucepan and stir over low heat until all the sugar and salt is dissolved. Allow to cool to room temperature.

3   Transfer the hot rice to a very large bowl. Fan the rice to drive off any excess moisture and gradually add the vinegar mixture, sprinkling it over the rice a little at a time and stirring the rice using a spatula in a cutting motion. Continue until the rice reaches body temperature. Test this by touching the rice with the back of your hand. It should feel very slightly warm to the touch. Cover with a clean cloth dampened with the vinegar mixture and set aside.

4   Cut each sheet of nori into quarters. Arrange your choice of fillings on a platter and serve with the rice, nori, wasabi, pickled ginger and soy sauce.

5   To eat, place a little rice on the rough side of a piece of nori and add the fillings you like. Fold or roll into a cone and eat.

≫ You don't need to shape these into cones when you eat them. We most often just fold the seaweed around the filling like a taco or roll it up a bit like a cigar.

SERVES 4 **PREPARATION TIME** 30 MINS **COOKING TIME** 20 MINS

SALMON SUSHI BALLS

サーモンの手毬寿司

LEARNING HOW TO HAND-MOULD SUSHI CAN TAKE A LIFETIME, AND MOST JAPANESE DON'T
EVEN TRY. HAND-ROLLED AND BALLED SUSHI ARE THE MOST POPULAR TYPES TO MAKE AT HOME.
GIVE IT A TRY. YOU DON'T NEED A BAMBOO MAT OR ANYTHING. JUST GRAB A PIECE OF PLASTIC
WRAP. WE MAKE THESE FOR OUR KIDS ALL THE TIME.

INGREDIENTS

300g sashimi-grade salmon
1 tsp wasabi (optional)
4 cups cooked Sushi Rice
   (see recipe on page 68)
2 tbsp Japanese mayonnaise
Boosted Soy Sauce (page 28),
   to serve
1 tsp finely chopped chives
½ avocado, thinly sliced
1 tsp salmon roe
Pickled ginger, to serve

METHOD

1 Basic method: Slice the salmon into very thin slices. Place a
slice of salmon in the centre of a large piece of plastic wrap. If using
wasabi, wipe a small amount onto the salmon using your finger. Top
with about 2 tbsp sushi rice. Gather the plastic wrap around the
rice and twist to form a firm ball shape about 5cm in diameter with
the salmon covering the top half of the rice. Unfurl the plastic wrap.

2 Make more rice balls using the same process, but with a few
variations:

· Torch the salmon with a blowtorch.
· Drizzle with a little Japanese mayonnaise and scatter with chives.
· Brush the salmon slices with Boosted Soy Sauce.
· Lay a slice or two of avocado on the plastic wrap first before
  placing the salmon and rice on top.
· Top the salmon with a few balls of salmon roe.

≫ This recipe includes a bunch of different ways to dress up salmon,
but you could easily use a variety of seafood instead.

SERVES 4 **PREPARATION TIME** 15 MINS **COOKING TIME** 0 MINS

NABEYAKI CHICKEN AND EGG UDON

鍋焼き親子うどん

RAMEN MAY HAVE ITS DEVOTEES FROM TOKYO TO NEW YORK, BUT THERE'S FAR MORE TO JAPANESE NOODLES. THIS UDON DISH IS BEST MADE IN INDIVIDUAL CLAYPOTS, BUT IF YOU DON'T HAVE ANY YOU CAN JUST DO THIS IN A NORMAL SAUCEPAN AND DIVIDE IT BETWEEN BOWLS TO SERVE.

INGREDIENTS

500g frozen udon noodles
2 spinach plants, washed
150g shimeji mushrooms, trimmed and broken into clumps
2 fresh shiitake mushrooms
2 chicken thigh fillets, cut into 2cm slices
6 snow peas, dethreaded
2 eggs
2 thin spring onions, finely sliced, to serve
½ tsp shichimi togarashi, to serve (optional)

STOCK

750ml All-purpose Chicken Dashi (page 31)
2 tbsp sake
¼ cup soy sauce
¼ cup mirin
½ tsp salt

METHOD

1 Bring a medium saucepan of water to the boil and blanch the noodles until separated, about 1 minute. Drain, rinse in cold running water then drain well. Bring the saucepan of water to the boil again and blanch the spinach plants for 30 seconds. Rinse in cold running water until cool enough to handle, then gather the plants together and squeeze out as much water as you can. Cut the spinach into 5cm lengths and discard the roots.

2 Divide the noodles, mushrooms and chicken between two small claypots. In a separate saucepan bring the ingredients for the stock to a simmer. Divide the hot stock between the claypots and place them over medium heat. Cover and bring to a simmer. Simmer for 1 minute, then add the snow peas and spinach, cover and simmer for a further minute. Then add the eggs (1 per pot) and simmer, covered, for 1 more minute. Scatter with the spring onions and shichimi togarashi, if using, to serve.

≫ This dish is often served with a single piece of prawn tempura on top, so feel free to add one if you're feeling especially energetic.

SERVES 2 **PREPARATION TIME** 15 MINS **COOKING TIME** 15 MINS

chapter soup and four nabemono

Soup is almost as ubiquitous as rice in Japanese cuisine. There is rarely a meal that passes in Japan without a soup.

Despite being so common, Japanese soups are tiny works of culinary art in themselves. Ingredients and vessels are chosen to reflect the seasons, and flavours, aromas and even the density of ingredients are delicately balanced so that some ingredients rise to the top while others sink to the bottom, creating an experience that changes from the first sip to the last.

Nabemono are soup's closest cousins. Literally meaning 'pot things', nabemono are a family of dishes that generally start with a flavoured broth that is used to cook raw ingredients right at the family dining table. It's a wonderful way to eat. Preparation takes very little time and every member of the family is involved in the cooking, chatting away and negotiating the strategy of what ingredients should be added when and who gets to eat what. Some of our family's happiest moments have taken place around a nabe.

CHILLED CORN AND SOY MILK SOUP

豆乳コーンスープ

THIS MODERN CHILLED SOUP IS QUITE POPULAR IN SUMMER IN JAPAN'S NORTHERNMOST
ISLAND, HOKKAIDO, WHICH IS KNOWN FOR ITS CORN AND POTATOES.

INGREDIENTS

4 ears of corn

1 litre All-purpose Chicken
  Dashi (page 31), or water

2 tbsp butter

1 medium potato, peeled and
  grated

1 medium onion, peeled and
  grated

600ml unsweetened soy milk,
  plus extra for garnish

½ tsp salt

2 tbsp finely chopped chives,
  to serve

METHOD

1 Holding the ears of corn vertically on a cutting board, use a
knife to strip the kernels from the cob. Reserve the kernels. Bring
the dashi to a simmer in a small saucepan and add the cobs.
Simmer, covered, for 30 minutes, then discard the cobs, reserving
the liquid.

2 Heat another small saucepan over medium heat and add the
butter, potato, onion and corn kernels. Sauté for 5 minutes until the
potato and onion are softened, then add the corn stock and simmer
for 15 minutes. Remove from the heat and allow to cool to room
temperature.

3 Transfer the contents of the saucepan to a blender and blend
to a smooth paste. Add the soy milk gradually and continue to
blend. Chill in the fridge for at least 1 hour. Season to taste with
salt, scatter with chives and splash on a little extra soy milk
before serving.

≫ Chilling a soup like this can change the seasoning required, as the
balance of tastes can be different to when it's warm. Taste the cold
soup and then adjust the seasoning to your liking.

SERVES 4 **PREPARATION TIME** 20 MINS **COOKING TIME** 1 HOUR, PLUS 1 HOUR CHILLING

1 Tofu and Mushroom Miso Soup
2 Cherry Tomato Miso Soup
3 Classic Clam Miso Soup
4 Potato and Onion Miso Soup

CLASSIC CLAM MISO SOUP

あさりの味噌汁

THE INGREDIENTS USED HERE ARE SOME OF THE MOST POPULAR FOR MAKING MISO SOUP,
AND THEY ARE CHOSEN AS MUCH FOR THEIR PRESENTATION AS THEY ARE FOR THEIR FLAVOUR.
INGREDIENTS FOR MISO SOUP SHOULD REMAIN SEPARATE AND, IDEALLY, SIT AT DIFFERENT LEVELS
WITHIN THE SOUP. THE CLAMS SIT AT THE BOTTOM, THE TOFU AND WAKAME OCCUPY THE MIDDLE
OF THE SOUP AND THE SPRING ONIONS FLOAT ON TOP. MISO SOUP ISN'T A SINGLE HOMOGENOUS
SOUP, BUT A SINGLE DISH USED TO PRESENT A VARIETY OF INGREDIENTS WITHIN IT.

INGREDIENTS

5g wakame (optional)
250g small clams, scrubbed
¼ cup sake
1 litre water
150g silken tofu, drained,
   pressed and cut into 2cm
   cubes
¼ cup light miso
2 thin spring onions, finely
   sliced to serve

METHOD

1   If using, rinse the wakame in tap water and place in a bowl,
covering with additional tap water and allowing to stand for around
10 minutes until softened, then cut into 2cm lengths.

2   Place the clams in a small saucepan over medium heat and
add the sake. Bring the sake to the boil and add the water. When
the clams are open and the liquid is simmering, add the tofu and
wakame and turn off the heat. Place the miso in a small strainer or
large ladle, submerge it into the liquid and stir it within the strainer
or ladle until the miso is dissolved. Discard any pieces of bran
solids left in the strainer. Stir through the spring onions and serve
immediately in individual bowls.

≫ Different types of miso can be used to create different flavours in soup.
Lighter coloured miso will generally be lighter in flavour, while miso that
has a more red colour and contains a higher proportion of soybeans will
be more strongly flavoured. You can even blend miso pastes together to
get the flavour you want.

SERVES 4   **PREPARATION TIME** 10 MINS   **COOKING TIME** 5 MINS

CHERRY TOMATO MISO SOUP

プチトマトの味噌汁

THIS VERSION MATCHES THE UMAMI AND SWEETNESS OF TOMATOES WITH RICH RED MISO
IN A MIXTURE OF BONITO STOCK AND WATER. IT'S A STRONGLY FLAVOURED SOUP THAT
WOULD MATCH WELL SERVED WITH HEAVIER, MEATIER DISHES.

INGREDIENTS

2 cups red cherry tomatoes
2 tbsp finely sliced spring
   onions
500ml Bonito Stock (page 30)
500ml water
¼ cup red miso

METHOD

1   Place the cherry tomatoes in a heatproof bowl and pour boiling water over to cover them. Allow to stand in the water for 30 seconds, then drain and peel with your fingers. Divide the tomatoes between four small bowls and scatter with the spring onions.

2   Bring the Bonito Stock and water to a simmer in a small saucepan over medium heat. Place the miso in a small strainer or large ladle, submerge it into the liquid and stir it within the strainer or ladle until the miso is dissolved. Discard any pieces of bran solids left in the strainer. Ladle the soup over the tomato and spring onions and serve.

≫ Miso soup should always be drunk straight from the bowl. You don't need a spoon. Use chopsticks to pick the individual ingredients out of the soup to eat.

SERVES 4   **PREPARATION TIME** 5 MINS   **COOKING TIME** 5 MINS

TOFU AND MUSHROOM MISO SOUP

豆腐とキノコの味噌汁

CHOOSE SEASONAL INGREDIENTS FOR YOUR MISO SOUP. THIS TOFU AND MUSHROOM VERSION
WOULD BE PERFECT FOR AUTUMN, SERVED WITH SALT-GRILLED SALMON (PAGE 122).

INGREDIENTS

1 litre water
2 dried shiitake mushrooms
100g shimeji mushrooms,
    broken into clumps
2–3 tbsp brown miso
100g silken tofu, drained,
    pressed and cut into 1cm
    square strips

METHOD

1   Bring the water to the boil in a small saucepan and
remove from the heat. Add the shiitake mushrooms and steep
for 20 minutes. Remove the mushrooms and discard the stalks.
Slice the caps into thin slices and return to the liquid with the
shimeji mushrooms. Bring to a simmer and simmer for 3 minutes
until the shimeji mushrooms are tender. Place the miso in a small
strainer or large ladle, submerge it into the liquid and stir it within
the strainer or ladle until the miso is dissolved. Discard any pieces
of bran solids left in the strainer. Remove the clumps of shimeji
mushroom from the pot and place in serving bowls with the tofu.
Ladle over the soup and serve immediately.

≫ Silken tofu is very delicate and can break apart if handled too much.
Press it by wrapping it in paper towel and placing a plate on top for
about 15 minutes. When adding the pressed tofu to the soup, place the
block of tofu in the palm of your hand and cut it carefully while you hold
it. Then you can gently drop it into the soup without it breaking.

SERVES 4 **PREPARATION TIME** 10 MINS **COOKING TIME** 10 MINS

POTATO AND ONION MISO SOUP

じゃが芋と玉ねぎの味噌汁

WHEN MAKING MISO SOUP, YOU NEED TO CONSIDER THE BALANCE BETWEEN THREE ELEMENTS:
THE STOCK, INGREDIENTS AND MISO. IN THIS SOUP, SIMMERING THE POTATO AND ONION WILL
ADD SWEETNESS TO THE STRONG BONITO STOCK, AND SO SLIGHTLY LESS MISO WILL BE NEEDED.

INGREDIENTS

2 medium potatoes, peeled
  and cut into chunks
1 small onion, cut into wedges
1 litre Bonito Stock (page 30)
2 tbsp brown miso

METHOD

1 Place the potatoes in cold water and soak for 15 minutes then
drain. Place the potatoes and onion in a medium saucepan and
cover with the Bonito Stock. Bring to a simmer and simmer for
10 minutes until the potato is tender. A sharp knife inserted into
the potato should come out easily.

2 Place the miso in a small strainer or large ladle, submerge it
into the liquid and stir it within the strainer or ladle until the miso
is dissolved. Discard any pieces of bran solids left in the strainer.
Ladle the soup into four bowls and serve immediately.

≫ Soaking the potatoes in cold water will remove excess starch and
avoid clouding the soup.

SERVES 4 **PREPARATION TIME** 10 MINS **COOKING TIME** 10 MINS

HAPUKA AND SHIITAKE CLEAR SOUP

ハプカと椎茸のお吸い物

THERE IS A MAGNIFICENT VARIETY OF SOUPS IN JAPANESE CUISINE EXTENDING FAR BEYOND MISO SOUP. THEY REFLECT THE SEASONS AND THE LOCAL INGREDIENTS THEY BRING, WHICH IS WHY MOST NEVER MAKE IT OUTSIDE JAPAN. HOWEVER, THE SAME LOCAL FLAVOUR THAT MAKES THEM QUINTESSENTIALLY JAPANESE, MAKES THEM SIMPLE TO RECREATE ABROAD. USE INGREDIENTS THAT ARE LOCAL TO YOU AND FOLLOW THE SIMPLE FORMULA BELOW.

INGREDIENTS

2 dried shiitake mushrooms
1.5 litres Bonito Stock
  (page 30)
4 small fillets hapuka
  (80–100g each)
1 tbsp sake
1 tsp salt
150g silken tofu, pressed
  (see page 82)
4 small strips lemon rind

METHOD

1 Rinse the mushrooms under cold water and bring the stock to the boil. Remove the stock from the heat, add the mushrooms and allow to stand for 20 minutes. Remove the mushrooms from the stock, trim and discard the stems, and thinly slice the caps.

2 Pour boiling water over the hapuka fillets and drain well.

3 Bring the stock back to a simmer and add the sake, salt and sliced shiitake. Gently add the fish and slowly simmer over low heat for just 5 minutes until the fish is cooked through. Skim any scum from the surface of the soup. Add the tofu and heat through.

4 Arrange the fish, tofu and shiitake in each bowl and ladle over a little of the soup. Top with a strip of lemon rind and close the lid of the soup bowl to retain the lemon aroma for serving.

≫ All clear Japanese soups will contain four principal elements: a flavourful clear broth, made in this case with bonito stock with a complication of shiitake and sake; a single main ingredient known as a *wan-dane* (here, the hapuka); a few supporting ingredients known as *wan-zuma* (the shiitake and tofu); and finally an aromatic or spicy high note called *sui-kuchi* (provided here by the lemon rind).

SERVES 4 PREPARATION TIME 15 MINS **COOKING TIME** 20 MINS

CHICKEN AND NOODLE CLEAR SOUP

ささみと春雨のお吸い物

EVEN THOUGH THIS SOUP CONTAINS NOODLES, IT'S NOT INTENDED AS A MAIN DISH. WITH
THE EXCEPTION OF SOME LARGER SOUP-NOODLE DISHES LIKE RAMEN AND UDON SOUPS,
SMALLER SOUPS LIKE THIS ARE INTENDED AS ACCOMPANIMENTS. THE NOODLES HERE PLAY
THE ROLE OF TEXTURE, AND AREN'T THERE TO FILL YOU UP.

INGREDIENTS

2 chicken tenderloins

1 carrot, cut into very fine
matchsticks

5cm small daikon, cut into
very fine matchsticks

2 fresh shiitake mushrooms,
very thinly sliced

2 spring onions, cut into very
fine matchsticks

100g dried mung bean noodles
(glass noodles)

½ tsp shichimi togarashi

SOUP STOCK

1 litre All-purpose Chicken
Dashi (page 31)

2 tbsp sake

1 tsp soy sauce

½ tsp salt

METHOD

1   Combine the ingredients for the soup stock and bring to a
simmer. Add the chicken and vegetables and simmer over very,
very low heat for about 7 minutes until the chicken is just cooked
through and the vegetables are tender. Skim any scum from the
top of the soup. Adjust the seasoning of the broth if necessary.

2   Bring a separate saucepan of water to the boil and boil the
noodles until tender. Drain well and trim into 5cm lengths.

3   Remove the chicken from the soup and thinly slice. Place a
mound of noodles in each serving bowl and place some of the
vegetables next to it. Arrange a few pieces of chicken there as well.
Ladle over as much of the soup broth as you like and sprinkle with
a little shichimi togarashi.

≫ In this soup an already-flavourful stock is boosted by gently cooking
the ingredients in it. The chicken provides the main element (*wan-dane*)
with the noodles and vegetables the supporting cast (*wan-zuma*). The
sprinkling of seven-spice chilli provides an aromatic flourish at the end
(*sui-kuchi*).

SERVES 4   **PREPARATION TIME** 20 MINS   **COOKING TIME** 15 MINS

医食同源

Isshoku dougen

Medicine and food have the same origin.

This proverb holds two meanings, and both are important. The first is obvious, the second a little more hidden.

The first meaning acknowledges the fundamental relationship between food and health. It's something so apparent and universal that we all already know it. We are what we eat. We take air with every breath, liquid with every sip and food with every bite. The food we eat has a monumental impact on our health.

However, because it's so obvious, we're also at risk of taking it for granted. Many of us wish we ate better – I certainly do, myself – so then why is it so hard to put into practice?

Perhaps it's a problem not of the message but the messengers. We get it from every corner – from every package we walk past in the supermarket, every commercial on television, every banner ad in the margins of every website, and every magazine that tells us that we can get our beach bodies ready for summer in just twelve weeks. We hear people, companies and products telling us how we should eat so often that eventually when we sit down in front of our doctor and they tell us we have to start eating more healthily, we hardly listen because we've heard it all before. Just one more voice in an already confusing rabble of lies, half-truths and, yes, some truths as well.

This is where the second, more hidden meaning of the proverb is all important.

Food and medicine may have the same origin, but they are not the same thing. Medicine is a set of rules, a strict regimen to follow on the advice of professionals. Food is something quite different. It's something we build a relationship with, something we share with others, something we use to celebrate, and that we learn from those closest to us, and teach in return as well.

Treating your food as if it were only medicine sucks the joy from it and confuses what food really is. But ignoring its relationship with our health is a very foolish thing indeed.

SHABU-SHABU

しゃぶしゃぶ

THE BEST THING ABOUT DISHES LIKE SHABU-SHABU THAT ARE COOKED AT THE TABLE IS NOT JUST THE EASE OF PREPARATION OR THE FACT THAT EVERYONE CAN CHOOSE WHAT THEY LIKE TO EAT, IT'S THAT THE WHOLE FAMILY IS INVOLVED IN COOKING THE MEAL. EATING IS BEST WHEN THE FOOD ISN'T PRESENTED ON A PEDESTAL. EATING IS BEST WHEN IT'S SHARED IN EVERY RESPECT.

INGREDIENTS

1 small square kombu,
  or 1 large dried scallop
2 tbsp sake
2 litres water
300g pork belly, thinly sliced
300g wagyu beef, thinly sliced
300g firm tofu, pressed and
  cut into 5cm cubes
¼ head Chinese cabbage, cut
  into 5cm slices
1 carrot, thinly sliced
1 small bunch edible
  chrysanthemum leaves, or
  blanched spinach
5 thick spring onions, sliced
  sharply diagonally
150g shimeji mushrooms
150g enoki mushrooms
250g frozen udon noodles,
  thawed and separated
1 cup Sesame Sauce
  (page 103)
1 cup Ponzu (page 102)

METHOD

1 Place the kombu (or dried scallop), sake and water in a wide casserole dish and bring to a simmer on the dining table using a tabletop gas or electric element. Arrange all the ingredients on a large platter, or a number of large platters. Divide the sauces into individual portions.

2 Load a few vegetables into the pot and bring to a simmer again. When the water is simmering, pick up a piece of meat with chopsticks and swish it through the liquid until just barely cooked. Dip in the sauce of your choice and eat immediately. With a fine wire sieve or wide ladle, frequently skim any scum forming on the surface. Continue at a leisurely pace, cooking and eating more meat as you like until the vegetables are finished. Reload the pot with vegetables and bring to a simmer again.

3 When nearly finished, the stock will have taken on the flavour of the meat and vegetables. Add the noodles and cook until to your liking.

≫ The name *shabu-shabu* is onomatopoeia for the sound the sliced meat makes as it's swished through the stock.

SERVES 4 **PREPARATION TIME** 20 MINS **COOKING TIME** 10 MINS

SUKIYAKI OF BEEF AND ASIAN GREENS

すき焼

ALONG WITH SHABU-SHABU, SUKIYAKI WITH ITS SWEET-SAVOURY MEATINESS IS ONE OF THE MOST POPULAR MEAT DISHES IN JAPANESE CUISINE. THIS RECIPE IS FOR SUKIYAKI IN THE KANSAI STYLE FROM THE AREA AROUND OSAKA, WHERE THE BEEF INGREDIENTS ARE BRIEFLY FRIED TO CREATE A STRONGER CARAMELISED FLAVOUR BEFORE THE *WARISHITA* SEASONING IS ADDED. AROUND TOKYO'S KANTO REGION, THE SEASONING IS ADDED FIRST AND THE MEAT IS SIMMERED IN IT FOR A MORE DELICATE FLAVOUR.

INGREDIENTS

1 tsp lard or vegetable oil
6 thick spring onions, sliced
   on a sharp diagonal
500g thinly sliced wagyu beef
300g firm tofu, preferably
   grilled
¼ Chinese cabbage, cut into
   2cm pieces
3 small green pak choy, cut
   into quarters
150g enoki mushrooms,
   trimmed
8 fresh shiitake mushrooms
300g shirataki noodles (thin
   konnyaku noodles)
1 cup Bonito Stock (page 30)
1 bunch spinach, blanched,
   drained, cut into 5cm lengths
1 bunch edible chrysanthemum
   leaves (optional)
4 eggs, beaten, to serve
   (optional)

WARISHITA SEASONING
¼ cup soy sauce
¼ cup sake
¼ cup sugar

METHOD

1 For the *warishita* seasoning, mix together the soy sauce, sake and sugar and stir to dissolve the sugar.

2 Heat the lard or vegetable oil in a large frying pan or paella pan over medium heat. Add the spring onions and lightly fry to flavour the oil, then move to one side of the pan. Add the beef and fry until browned then move to one side of the pan. Add the tofu, cabbage, pak choy, mushrooms and shirataki noodles in separate piles and lightly fry, then add the *warishita* seasoning mix. Bring to a simmer, adding a little of the Bonito Stock as you go so that it doesn't get too dry. Add the spinach and chrysanthemum leaves, if using, after everything else is cooked.

3 Eat by dipping the hot meat in beaten raw egg just before it goes into your mouth. If that's not your thing (and I must admit it's not mine), just skip the raw egg (like I do).

≫ Traditional sukiyaki uses fewer vegetables and adds extra ingredients like *kuruma-fu* (wheel-shaped wheat gluten) and edible chrysanthemum leaves. In Australia these ingredients are not always available, so we use Asian greens instead.

SERVES 4 **PREPARATION TIME** 15 MINS **COOKING TIME** 20 MINS

SOY MILK NABE

豆乳鍋

THE KEY TO THIS DISH IS TO USE A STRONG STOCK SO THAT IT REMAINS FLAVOURFUL EVEN WHEN DILUTED WITH THE SOY MILK. AS THE MEAL PROGRESSES, THE STOCK WILL TAKE ON MORE AND MORE FLAVOUR AND BY THE END, IT'LL BE THE TASTIEST SOUP YOU'VE EVER HAD.

INGREDIENTS

750ml All-purpose Chicken Dashi (page 31)
500ml unsweetened soy milk
1 tsp salt
½ tsp sesame oil
400g pork belly, thinly sliced
200g chicken thigh fillet, thinly sliced
1 bunch spinach, blanched and drained
½ Chinese cabbage, quartered lengthways and cut into 5cm slices
4 large spring onions, sliced on the diagonal into 5cm pieces
1 bunch garlic chives, cut into 7cm lengths
300g enoki mushrooms, trimmed
150g beansprouts
300g silken tofu, cut into 2cm cubes

METHOD

1 Mix the dashi, soy milk, salt and sesame oil together in a wide, lidded pot. Arrange the sliced meat, vegetables and tofu on a large platter.

2 Place the pot over a tabletop gas burner or stove on medium heat and bring to a simmer. Add the ingredients to the pot at the table a little at a time and simmer until cooked.

≫ For a more impressive presentation, you can arrange the ingredients in the pot first, then pour the soup over and bring to the boil at the table. Blanching the spinach first stops it from colouring the soup when it's cooked.

SERVES 4 **PREPARATION TIME** 20 MINS **COOKING TIME** 10 MINS

TANTAN CHICKEN NABE

鶏坦々鍋

TANTAN (OR *DAN-DAN*) NOODLES IN CHINA ARE USUALLY MADE WITH BEEF, BUT IN JAPAN THE SPICY SESAME SOUP BASE IS GIVEN A LITTLE MORE ROOM TO PLAY. THE NOODLES WITH BEEF ARE STILL A FAVOURITE AT *RAMEN-YA*, BUT AT HOME AND AS A NABE, ANYTHING GOES.

INGREDIENTS

600g thinly sliced chicken
    thigh fillets
½ Chinese cabbage, halved
    again lengthways and cut into
    5cm slices
6 thick spring onions, sliced on
    the diagonal into 5cm pieces
6 fresh shiitake mushrooms,
    stalks removed
1 bunch garlic chives, cut into
    5cm lengths
300g enoki mushrooms,
    trimmed
300g silken tofu, cut into
    2cm cubes

TANTAN BASE

1 tsp Sichuan peppercorns
1 tbsp sesame oil
4 cloves garlic, grated
5cm ginger, grated
1 tsp Korean chilli powder
½ cup tahini
½ tsp salt
1 tsp sugar
2 tbsp black vinegar
2 tbsp mirin
2 tbsp sake
2 tbsp soy sauce
1 litre All-purpose Chicken
    Dashi (page 31)
1 tbsp chilli oil (optional)

METHOD

1   For the *tantan* base, toast the Sichuan peppercorns, and grind them to a fine powder. Heat the sesame oil in a saucepan over medium heat and fry the garlic and ginger until fragrant. Add the chilli powder and peppercorn powder and stir to combine. Add the remaining ingredients and bring to a simmer. Simmer for 15 minutes. Using a stick blender, blend the base to a smooth, creamy soup and adjust for seasoning. The soup should be a little bitter but if it's too bitter for your taste, add a little rice vinegar.

2   Arrange about half the ingredients in the nabe pot and pour over the soup. Arrange the remaining ingredients on a serving platter. Bring the soup to a simmer at the table, skimming any scum that rises to the top. As you finish eating the ingredients, you can add extra into the pot.

≫ Finishing this nabe with rice and egg makes for a delicious rice porridge that tastes a little like a spicy sesame risotto. Trust me, it's much better than it sounds. Just add a couple of cups of cooked rice and a couple of raw eggs to any soup left over in the dish. Continue to heat until the egg sets, then eat.

SERVES 4   **PREPARATION TIME** 30 MINS   **COOKING TIME** 30 MINS

chapter japanese
five salads

Salads as we know them are relatively recent additions to Japanese cuisine. There have been dishes of mixed cooked or raw vegetables forever, but their assembly into a single serving dish is a function of post-Meiji era influence from abroad. It's a good thing, too, as Japanese cuisine has taken to salads like a duck to water.

What sets many Japanese salads apart are their umami-rich dressings. While a traditional vinaigrette might have a balance of salty, sweet and sour tastes, Japanese dressings are often seasoned with soy sauce, mirin, toasty sesame oil or even miso, bringing to bear a strong savoury element that salads can sometimes lack. For a light meal or side dish, you could do a lot worse.

1 Wa-fu Dressing
2 Ginger Dressing
3 Sesame Sauce
4 Miso Dressing
5 Ponzu
6 Onion and Garlic Vinaigrette

PONZU

ポン酢

AS A DRESSING OR SAUCE, PONZU IS AT HOME ANYWHERE. DIP MEAT AND VEGETABLES INTO IT, POUR IT OVER A SALAD, OR SERVE IT WITH A STEAK. YOU WONT REGRET MAKING A LITTLE EXTRA TO KEEP ON HAND.

INGREDIENTS

75ml sake
75ml mirin
¼ tsp caster sugar
150ml light soy sauce
75ml freshly squeezed
    lemon juice

METHOD

1 Bring the sake, mirin and sugar to a simmer in a small saucepan. Simmer for 1 minute, stir in the soy sauce and return to a simmer. Remove from the heat and stir in the lemon juice. Cool and store in fridge for up to 2 weeks.

≫ The name 'ponzu' translates to 'a sour punch' and it's defined by the balance between the savoury soy sauce and the sour citrus.

MAKES 1½ CUPS **PREPARATION TIME** 5 MINS **COOKING TIME** 5 MINS

ONION AND GARLIC VINAIGRETTE

玉ねぎとニンニクのドレッシング

THE ONION ADDS BODY TO THIS DRESSING, HELPING IT STICK TO SALAD INGREDIENTS, THE PUNGENCY OF RAW ONION THAT MAKES YOU CRY WHEN YOU CUT IT GIVES THE DRESSING A LOVELY GENTLE SPICINESS.

INGREDIENTS

1 small onion (preferably white,
    but you can use a brown
    onion)
2 cloves garlic
2 tbsp caster sugar
¼ cup soy sauce
¼ cup rice vinegar
¼ tsp freshly ground black
    pepper
½ cup grapeseed oil

METHOD

1 Finely grate the onion and garlic on a Japanese grater. If you don't have a Japanese grater, mince them very finely with a knife. Combine with the sugar, soy sauce, rice vinegar and pepper, and whisk lightly to combine and dissolve the sugar. You don't want to emulsify this dressing as it may become too thick. Add the oil all at once and rest in the fridge for a few hours to mellow. Shake before use.

≫ White onions have a sweeter and less pungent taste than brown onions, which makes them perfect for this dressing.

MAKES ABOUT 1½ CUPS **PREPARATION TIME** 10 MINS **COOKING TIME** 0 MINS

SESAME SAUCE

胡麻だれ

ALONG WITH PONZU, THIS SESAME SAUCE IS ONE OF THE MOST VERSATILE
IN JAPANESE CUISINE. IT'S OFTEN SERVED TOGETHER WITH PONZU FOR
DISHES LIKE SHABU-SHABU (PAGE 90).

INGREDIENTS

½ cup white sesame seeds
2 tbsp sake
2 tbsp mirin
1 tbsp caster sugar
¼ cup soy sauce
1 tbsp rice vinegar
¼ cup sesame oil

METHOD

1   Toast the sesame seeds by placing them in a small dry
saucepan over medium heat. Swirl the saucepan to stir until the
seeds are golden brown and fragrant then remove from the pan
and set aside. Return the saucepan to the heat and add the sake
and mirin and bring to the boil, then remove from the heat.

2   Add the caster sugar to the sesame seeds and grind to a
smooth paste. Add the sake, mirin, soy sauce, rice vinegar, sesame
oil and 1–2 tbsp cold water and continue to grind to a smooth and
creamy sauce. This sauce can be used as is for dishes like Shabu-
shabu (page 90) or Steamed Pork with Sesame Sauce (page 150)
or mixed into other preparations like:

SESAME DRESSING
Mix the base sesame sauce 3:1:1 with rice vinegar and water
(e.g. 3 tbsp sesame sauce with 1 tbsp vinegar and 1 tbsp water).

SESAME MAYONNAISE
Mix the base sesame sauce 1:1 with Japanese mayonnaise.

≫ Toasting sesame seeds brings out their flavour and makes them easier
to grind, particularly if you're using a Japanese mortar and pestle (page 9).

MAKES ABOUT 1½ CUPS **PREPARATION TIME** 10 MINS **COOKING TIME** 10 MINS

WA-FU DRESSING

和風ドレッシング

WA-FU MEANS 'JAPANESE-STYLE' AND IN A FOOD CONTEXT IT'S USED TO DESCRIBE
A FOREIGN FOOD THAT'S BEEN ADAPTED IN A JAPANESE WAY. THIS COULD BE PASTA,
HAMBURGERS, STEWS, OR IN THIS CASE A VINAIGRETTE. ALTHOUGH THE MEANING OF
WA-FU IN THIS CONTEXT IS VERY WELL UNDERSTOOD, THE LITERAL TRANSLATION OF
ITS CHARACTERS READS AS 'HARMONIOUS WIND', WHICH I THINK IS QUITE POETIC.

INGREDIENTS

2 tbsp soy sauce
2 tbsp rice vinegar
2 tbsp cold water
1 tbsp sugar
1 tsp sesame oil
½ tsp toasted sesame seeds

METHOD

1 Combine all the ingredients and stir to dissolve the sugar.

≫ Wa-fu dressing is not emulsified like a Western vinaigrette and should
be shaken to distribute the sesame oil. If you prefer an oilier version,
add 2 tbsp grapeseed oil to this, as too much sesame oil will overwhelm
the flavour.

MAKES ABOUT ½ CUP **PREPARATION TIME** 2 MINS **COOKING TIME** 0 MINS

MISO DRESSING

味噌ドレッシング

THERE'S VERY LITTLE MISO CAN'T DO. ITS SAVOURY UMAMI TASTE IS BEST KNOWN
IN SOUPS, BUT IT CAN IMPROVE EVERYTHING FROM STIR-FRIES TO MARINADES
TO PICKLES, AND HERE IT POPS UP AGAIN AS A DRESSING.

INGREDIENTS

¼ cup light miso
2 tbsp water
¼ cup rice vinegar
2 tsp sugar
1 tbsp sesame oil
¼ cup grapeseed oil

METHOD

1 Mix the miso, water, vinegar and sugar together to a smooth
paste. Whisk in the sesame oil and then whisk in the grapeseed
oil a little at a time until fully combined.

≫ Just as with soups, different varieties of miso will produce different
characteristics in this dressing. Find a variety that suits your tastes.

MAKES ABOUT 1 CUP **PREPARATION TIME** 5 MINS **COOKING TIME** 0 MINS

GINGER DRESSING

生姜とハチミツのドレッシング

THE FLAVOUR OF GINGER IS ALMOST ALL IN ITS JUICE. WHEN YOU'RE GRATING
GINGER FOR THIS DRESSING OR ANY DISH, MAKE SURE YOU GRATE IT EITHER
DIRECTLY INTO THE DISH OR ONTO A PLATE RATHER THAN ONTO A CUTTING BOARD.
THIS WILL HELP YOU CAPTURE AS MUCH OF THE JUICE AS POSSIBLE.

INGREDIENTS

5cm ginger
1 tbsp soy sauce
¼ cup rice vinegar (preferably
  brown rice vinegar)
¼ tsp salt
1 tsp honey
½ cup olive oil

METHOD

1   Grate the ginger using a Japanese grater or rasp grater. Squeeze out and reserve the juice of the ginger using a piece of muslin or by squeezing the ginger between two spoons. Discard the solids.

2   Combine the ginger juice with the remaining ingredients in a jar and shake well.

≫ Japanese dressings always contain a source of umami (often soy sauce), giving them a more savoury taste than many Western dressings. This is a very important characteristic for getting the best flavour out of your salads. Even with Western dressings, a little chopped anchovy or a splash of fish sauce or soy sauce can work wonders.

MAKES ABOUT ¾ CUP **PREPARATION TIME** 10 MINS **COOKING TIME** 0 MINS

BUTASHABU SALAD

豚しゃぶサラダ

THE KEY TO THIS DISH IS HAVING THE PORK SLICED VERY FINELY. IT'S A STANDARD
CUT IN JAPAN BUT THINLY SLICED PORK BELLY CAN BE A LITTLE HARD TO FIND HERE.
IT'S AVAILABLE FROZEN FROM ASIAN GROCERS, OR FRESH FROM ASIAN BUTCHERS.
IF YOU DON'T HAVE AN ASIAN BUTCHER NEARBY, YOUR NORMAL BUTCHER MAY
SLICE IT FOR YOU BY HAND IF YOU ASK THEM VERY NICELY.

INGREDIENTS

1 tbsp sake

1 tsp salt

300g pork belly, very thinly
   sliced (around 2mm thick)

4 thick spring onions, finely
   shredded

2 cups mixed salad leaves

2 cups picked watercress

1 small Lebanese cucumber,
   cut into thin diagonal half-
   moons

2 cups mixed cherry tomatoes,
   halved

½ cup Sesame Dressing
   (page 103)

2 tbsp Japanese mayonnaise,
   to serve

METHOD

1 In a medium saucepan bring about 1 litre of water to a rolling
boil and add 1 tbsp sake and 1 tsp salt. Add half the pork to the
water and separate the pieces with a pair of chopsticks. Remove
from the water to a separate plate as soon as the pork turns
white and is cooked through. This will take just a minute or two,
depending on the thickness of the pork. Return the water to the boil
and repeat for the remaining pork.

2 Mix the spring onions, salad leaves, watercress, cucumber and
tomato together, and toss with half the dressing. Arrange on a plate
and top with the pork. Spoon the remaining dressing over the pork
and serve with a dollop of mayonnaise.

≫ If you can't buy pork belly cut thinly, chill the pork in the freezer for
an hour or so and use a very, very sharp knife to cut it yourself.

SERVES 2 **PREPARATION TIME** 15 MINS **COOKING TIME** 10 MINS

SASHIMI SALAD

刺身サラダ

THERE WAS PROBABLY A TIME WHEN A SASHIMI SALAD WOULD HAVE THROWN JAPANESE FOOD PURISTS INTO A CONNIPTION. SOME ARE PROBABLY SHAKING THEIR HEADS ABOUT IT RIGHT NOW. BUT THAT DOESN'T CHANGE THE FACT THAT THESE SALADS ARE SOME OF THE MOST POPULAR ITEMS AT CASUAL AND MODERN *IZAKAYAS* AROUND THE COUNTRY AND ALL OVER THE WORLD. THE TENDER FISH AND FRESH VEGETABLES ARE PERFECTLY OFFSET BY CRISPY SHREDS OF WONTON.

INGREDIENTS

About 2 litres oil, for deep-frying
6 wonton wrappers
300g mixed sashimi (kingfish, tuna and salmon)
1 small red onion, peeled and very finely sliced
4 cups mixed salad leaves
1 cup finely shredded daikon
1 cup snow pea shoots
½ cup Onion and Garlic Vinaigrette (page 102)

METHOD

1 Heat the oil to 200°C. Very thinly slice the wonton wrappers and deep-fry in batches for about 1 minute until crispy and lightly browned. Drain well.

2 Toss the sashimi, onion, salad leaves, daikon, snow pea shoots and about half the dressing together. Place in a mound on a plate and top with the remaining dressing and the wonton crisps.

≫ Some believe the rise of sashimi salads in Japan came about from the popularity of the *yee sang*, a modern raw fish salad that's become a Chinese New Year staple around Singapore and Malaysia – a dish that was originally inspired by Japanese sashimi. And so the wheel turns.

SERVES 2 **PREPARATION TIME** 15 MINS **COOKING TIME** 1 MIN

JAPANESE GARDEN SALAD

和風ガーデンサラダ

I DON'T KNOW WHY THE WHOLE WORLD HAS TAKEN SO LONG TO REALISE THAT CHOPSTICKS
ARE THE *PERFECT* SALAD EATING UTENSILS, BUT THEY REALLY ARE. MAKE THIS JAPANESE
SALAD AS A MIXTURE OF TEXTURES AND SHAPES, ARRANGED IN GROUPS RATHER THAN TOSSED
TOGETHER, AND THEN GRAB A PAIR OF CHOPSTICKS AND SLOWLY GRAZE YOUR WAY THROUGH IT.

INGREDIENTS

1 cup broccoli florets

1 ear of corn

2 eggs (or Soy-flavoured Eggs, page 178)

2 cups mixed salad leaves

4 cups cabbage, very finely shredded

1 carrot, cut into very fine matchsticks

2 thick spring onions, cut into very fine matchsticks

1 Lebanese cucumber, thinly sliced

2 tomatoes, cut into wedges

1 small red onion, cut into very thin rings

About ½ cup dressing of your choice (see pages 102–105)

METHOD

1 Bring a saucepan of water to the boil and boil the broccoli florets for just 1 minute until tender. Plunge in a bowl of cold water and drain well. Add the corn and simmer for about 8 minutes, then plunge in cold water, drain and strip the kernels from the cob using a sharp knife. Return the water to the boil and boil the eggs for 7½ minutes. Stand in cold water until cool enough to handle, then peel.

2 Arrange the salad ingredients in piles on a large platter. Serve with any of the dressings on pages 102–105.

≫ You can even serve this salad with a selection of dressings. Serve them on the side and add them as you pick the ingredients from the platter.

SERVES 4 **PREPARATION TIME** 20 MINS **COOKING TIME** 15 MINS

腹八分に
医者いらず

Harahachibu ni issha irazu

Eight-tenths full keeps the doctor away.

This is the Japanese version of 'an apple a day' and I have to say, as much as I love apples, it's a bit more useful in the modern day than just singing the praises of a single fruit.

'Eight-tenths full' (*harahachibu*) is the Japanese mantra of moderate eating, and it's been touted as the reason for many benefits, from the health of the Okinawans, whose traditional diet produced the longest-lived people in history, to the stereotypically slender Japanese figure.

What's most interesting about many of the messages around Japanese food and health is how they are reinforced culturally. An idiom like this warning against eating to excess is not just a recommendation for an individual, it's explaining a society-wide cultural taboo.

The modern world could fairly be described as one of excess. If there is something we don't have, we want it. If there is something we have a little of, we want more. Where does it end? In among all these wants and mores it can sometimes seem like gluttony is a virtue not a vice. At those times it can be nice to have some tried and true ancient wisdom to remind yourself that doesn't have to be the case.

CHICKEN, DAIKON AND CUCUMBER SALAD

鶏肉と大根ときゅうりの三色サラダ

THE SECRET TO MAKING THIS SALAD WELL IS TO KEEP THE SIZE OF THE INGREDIENTS CONSISTENT. IF YOU SHRED THE CHICKEN VERY FINELY, MAKE SURE YOU SHRED THE DAIKON AND CUCUMBER TO THE SAME SIZE. IF YOU LEAVE THE CHICKEN A LITTLE MORE COARSE, YOU CAN AFFORD TO DO SO WITH THE DAIKON AND CUCUMBER, TOO.

INGREDIENTS

1 chicken breast fillet
½ tsp salt
½ daikon, shredded and drained
1 Lebanese cucumber, shredded
½ cup Sesame Mayonnaise (page 103)
1 sheet nori

METHOD

1 For the chicken breast, bring a small saucepan of water to a very low simmer. Steam should rise from the water with just a few bubbles forming at the base of the pan. Add the whole fillet and continue to heat for just 2 minutes then cover tightly, remove from the heat and stand covered for a further 10 minutes. Remove the chicken breast, rub a little salt on your hands and finely shred the meat.

2 Combine with the daikon and cucumber and toss with the Sesame Mayonnaise. Wave the nori over an open gas flame until it is toasted and brittle. Crumble the nori over the salad and serve.

≫ You could even use a turning slicer (spiraliser) to make this salad. They were invented in Japan and have been used for years there before their recent worldwide boom in popularity.

SERVES 2 **PREPARATION TIME** 15 MINS **COOKING TIME** 15 MINS

'SPRING RAIN' NOODLE SALAD WITH SPINACH AND SHIITAKE

ほうれん草と椎茸の春雨サラダ

THE LOVELY, SLIGHTLY CHEWY GLASS NOODLES IN THIS DISH (CALLED 'SPRING RAIN' NOODLES IN JAPANESE) ARE PARTICULARLY GOOD AT CARRYING THE FLAVOUR OF SAUCES AND DRESSINGS. WE TEND TO TREAT THIS AS MORE OF A SIDE DISH THAN A MEAL, BUT YOU COULD ALWAYS BULK IT OUT A BIT WITH ADDITIONAL INGREDIENTS LIKE SHREDDED CHICKEN, HAM, CUCUMBER OR EGG.

INGREDIENTS

75g dried mung bean noodles
   (glass noodles)
1 small spinach plant
4 large fresh shiitake
   mushrooms, thinly sliced
1 small clove garlic, finely
   minced with a pinch of salt
¼ cup Sesame Dressing
   (page 103)
1 tsp toasted sesame seeds

METHOD

1   Bring a pot of water to the boil over high heat. Rinse the glass noodles in cold water then add to the boiling water. Boil for about 7 minutes until tender. Remove the noodles from the water and rinse in cold water until cooled. Drain well and cut through the mass of noodles a few times using a pair of scissors.

2   Blanch the spinach in boiling water for about 1 minute until tender. Rinse in cold water until cooled then squeeze out as much liquid as possible. Cut into 5cm lengths, discarding the roots. Boil the mushroom slices for about 30 seconds and drain well.

3   Combine the noodles, spinach, mushroom, garlic and dressing in a large bowl and toss to coat well. Transfer to a serving plate and scatter with sesame seeds to serve.

≫ Cutting the noodles makes them easier to eat. You don't need to be too fussy with it. A few snips with a pair of scissors will do the trick.

SERVES 2 **PREPARATION TIME** 15 MINS **COOKING TIME** 15 MINS

CARROT SALAD

人参サラダ

THIS SALAD WON'T BE A WHOLE MEAL, BUT IMAGINE THIS TOGETHER WITH A PIECE OF GRILLED FISH, A BOWL OF MISO SOUP AND A BOWL OF WHOLEGRAIN RICE (PAGE 52) AND THE JIGSAW OF JAPANESE CUISINE STARTS TO COME TOGETHER. SIMPLE AND EXPRESSIVE ELEMENTS ARRANGED TOGETHER INTO A MEAL THAT IS GREATER THAN THE SUM OF ITS PARTS.

INGREDIENTS

1 large carrot, lightly peeled
   and very finely shredded
Good pinch of salt
Handful of snow pea shoots
2 tbsp Ginger Dressing
   (page 105)

METHOD

1   Toss the carrot and the salt together, and allow to stand in a sieve over a bowl in the fridge for about 10 minutes. Then toss the carrot with the snow pea shoots and Ginger Dressing and serve.

≫ Salting vegetables in this way removes some of their moisture, taking their texture away from rawness but preserving the raw flavour. Sometimes 'cooking' is just as simple as that.

SERVES 2 **PREPARATION TIME** 10 MINS **COOKING TIME** 0 MINS

chapter
six fish

There are thousands of species of fish that fill the rivers and lakes of Japan, and the seas that surround it. Quite a few of those will make it onto Japanese dinner tables at some time or another. If you've ever wondered why a sushi master takes ten years to qualify to make a single mouthful of fish and rice, much of the training involves understanding the details and nuances of so many varieties.

Thankfully, for those of us who cook at home for our families, the learning curve is far less steep. With fish, as with all ingredients in Japanese cuisine, the key is simplicity. Fish is at its best when very little has been done to it, allowing its natural flavours to present themselves.

SHIOYAKI (salt-grilling)

塩焼き

FISH GRILLED WITH SALT. THERE REALLY ISN'T ANYTHING MORE TO IT THAN THAT, AND WHEN YOU THINK ABOUT IT THERE REALLY DOESN'T NEED TO BE. A WELL-GRILLED PIECE OF FISH IS DEFINED BY THE SWEET, MINERAL UMAMI OF THE DELICATE FLESH AND THE MORE A COOK GETS IN THE WAY OF THAT FLAVOUR THE MORE'S THE PITY.

There are thousands of varieties of seafood, all with their distinctive flavours and textures. Far more than the number of seasonings and flavourings we keep in our pantries. The goal of cooking fish in this style should be to present its flavours as simply and as faithfully as possible.

INGREDIENTS

Any kind of fish (see Selection and Preparation), either whole or in fillets
Fine salt

TO SERVE

Daikon, peeled and finely grated
Few slices of lemon
Boosted Soy Sauce (page 28) or Ponzu (page 102)
Grated ginger (optional)

SELECTION AND PREPARATION

Absolutely any fish can be prepared in the *shioyaki* style. Some of my favourites, whether as whole fish or fillets, include: snapper, sea bream, trout, salmon, mackerel and blue-eye trevalla. Your choice of fish should be dictated by what is available seasonally and locally.

Clean and scale the fish, including the head (the meat from around the jaw and cheek is some of the best). Prepare, skewer and season the fish with salt (see Skewering and Salting on pages 124–125).

For fillets, select fillets that look fresh and moist around the edges and which smell mineral rather than fishy. Ideally fillets should be scaled and boned, although it is not difficult to do this yourself when you get home.

Scale the fillets and remove any bones and thread the fillets onto 2–3 long skewers, if using (see Skewering on page 124), radiating from a point like a fan, as this will stop the fillets from spinning. Season the fish with fine salt from a height for even coverage (see Salting on page 125).

COOKING METHODS

BARBECUE OR COALS

Cooking over coals is the best way to cook *shioyaki*, but it's not always practical for home cooking. Japanese cooks favour *binchotan*, an oak charcoal that emits a high amount of infrared radiation, heating the fish beneath the surface for faster cooking and juicier results. You may be able to buy purpose-made fish grills from Japanese grocers for use on a gas stove (see page 9). They do a reasonable job of recreating the charcoal-grilled flavour indoors at home. You can tell when the fish is ready when the skewers pull easily out of the fish with a gentle twisting motion.

OVEN

A good oven can easily produce excellent *shioyaki*, particularly with whole fish like snapper. Heat your oven to its hottest temperature (fan-forced) and set the grill setting as well. Place the seasoned fish on a wire rack over a baking tray and bake until cooked through. A whole 30cm snapper takes about 20 minutes. You don't even have to flip it!

OVERHEAD GRILL

Japanese kitchens don't usually have ovens, but will have a small overhead grill used most often for cooking fish. For fillets you can choose to turn the fish or just grill one side only. For whole fish you may need to flip them, so grill the presentation side last.

FRYING PAN

Grilling or baking will produce the best results for *shioyaki*, but pan-frying can be a quick alternative. Use only a little oil – just enough to stop the fish from sticking to the pan – as you want the heat to be quite dry to intensify the flavour of the fish.

1 SKEWERING

When skewering whole ocean fish, use a technique known as 'wave skewering' (*uneri-gushi*) to make it easier to handle the fish while grilling, and to pose the fish for presentation as if it's still in motion. With one metal skewer, enter under the eye of the fish, coming out just behind the pectoral fin, bend the fish sharply and enter the fish again, emerging just before the tail. Repeat with another skewer at an angle to the first, creating a V-shape. This will stop the fish from spinning around the skewers as it cooks. The skewers should penetrate only one side of the fish, with the other side reserved for presentation. Slash a crossed grilling cut (*yakimono-bocho*) into the presentation side of the fish at the thickest part of the flesh to ensure it cooks evenly and to prevent the skin from shrinking and tearing.

2 SALTING

Use a fine salt to make it easier to ensure the fish is salted evenly. Heavily salting the fins of whole fish prevents them from scorching, but also looks attractive for presentation. Fresh fish should have enough moisture on its surface for the salt to adhere, but if the skin of your fish is a little dry, you can spray it with a little water or oil to help hold the salt, and also to help with the cooking process.

3 FILLETS

Fillets have their idiosyncrasies. They aren't supported by structural bones, so the flesh may shrink. They may also vary in thickness from one side to the other so that they cook unevenly. For barbecuing or charcoal grilling fillets can be skewered, but for pan-frying, oven baking or overhead grilling it may be easier just to leave them separate. While the goal of *shioyaki* is usually crisp skin, a warm chargrilled flavour and moist, tender flesh, a little dryness need not always be a disappointment. I actually prefer fish a little dry at times, particularly in many Japanese meals. Across a whole meal, a balance of flavours and textures is needed. The contrast between slightly dry but intensely flavoured fish with plump rice in one mouthful, and warm silken tofu in miso soup the next, can be a very pleasant experience.

4 ACCOMPANIMENTS

Like the grilling method, the accompaniments for salt-grilled fish tend to be kept minimal. The most popular (and my favourite) is *daikon-oroshi*, a mound of grated raw daikon stained with a few drops of soy sauce. A smaller pile of raw grated ginger is sometimes added for oilier fish, to cut through the fishy aroma. The fish can also be served with Ponzu (page 102) or even just a squeeze of fresh citrus, like a sudachi lime. If you prefer a little spiciness for strongly flavoured fish, you could replace the *daikon-oroshi* with a little Autumn-leaf Radish (page 154). For contrast and presentation, salt-grilled fish are often served on a plate lined with a green bamboo or shiso leaf.

MISOZUKE (miso-marinating)
味噌漬け

THIS PROCESS IS ONE OF THE MOST USEFUL IN JAPANESE COOKING. IT REQUIRES JUST
A FEW SEASONINGS AND IS AN EXTREMELY SIMPLE WAY TO PRODUCE DELICIOUS AND AUTHENTIC
RESULTS. THIS IS THE PROCESS THAT PRODUCES THE POPULAR MISO-MARINATED COD DISHES
AT HIGH-END JAPANESE RESTAURANTS OUTSIDE JAPAN, BUT WITHIN JAPAN THIS IS CONSIDERED
A SIMPLE HOME-COOKING TECHNIQUE. IT'S NOT JUST LIMITED TO FISH, EITHER. ONCE YOU HAVE
MADE YOUR *MISO-DOKO*, IT CAN BE STORED FOR A COUPLE OF WEEKS AND USED TO CURE AND
FLAVOUR ANY NUMBER OF INGREDIENTS.

INGREDIENTS

400g fish fillets (see Selection
   and Preparation)

MISO-DOKO

1 cup white miso
2 tbsp mirin
1 tbsp sake

TO SERVE

See Accompaniments
   (page 128)

SELECTION AND PREPARATION

Unlike *shioyaki*, *misozuke* is generally made with fillets rather than
whole fish. Firm, slightly fatty fish are best, but you can apply this
process to many different varieties. Some of my favourites include:
salmon, sea perch, pomfret, cod, tilefish and blue-eye trevalla. The
fish pictured here is Patagonian toothfish, which is excellent done
in this style.

Use scaled fillets, or you may wish to remove the skin altogether.
Unlike *shioyaki*, the skin of the fish will not necessarily crisp. It can
be eaten in any case, but it is just a matter of personal preference.

CURING

To prepare the curing mixture (*miso-doko*), mix the miso, mirin and sake together to a thick paste. Spread half of the paste over the base of a tray and cover with a layer of muslin. Place the fish on the muslin, then cover with another layer of muslin. Spread the remaining paste over the top layer of muslin to sandwich the fish inside. Cure the fish in the fridge for 24–48 hours. Wipe off any *miso-doko* remaining on the fish (I find it useful to scrape it off with a blunt knife first and then wipe away any residue with a damp cloth or paper towel.)

COOKING

Misozuke fish can be baked or grilled just as for *shioyaki*, although the direct heat of pan-frying may not be suitable. If cooking over coals you will not need oil, as the oil released by the fish should coat itself, but if baking or using an overhead grill a light brush with grapeseed oil will give the fish a nice shine and help it to cook more evenly. The exposed flesh of the fish should take on a burnished appearance.

ACCOMPANIMENTS

I have used a few blanched green beans here but you could also use a small wedge of lime or lemon, or a small amount of *daikon-oroshi* (page 125). A more traditional garnish is a colourful stalk of ginger pickled in plum vinegar, known as *yanaka-shouga*. This can be difficult to find so an acceptable substitute is a small pile of *gari* pickled ginger, the kind you might serve with sushi or sashimi.

1 MAKING THE *MISO-DOKO*
The *miso-doko* used for curing the fish is very simple to make, but there are a few rules to follow. Use a sweeter miso that has low salt content to avoid the cured food becoming too salty. You may sometimes see this style of curing and grilling referred to as *saikyo-yaki*. It is the same technique but just using *saikyo-miso*, a particular style of sweet miso from the Kansai region.

2 USING THE *MISO-DOKO*

Layering the ingredients between muslin makes them much easier to prepare for grilling, but it also helps preserve the volume of the *miso-doko* for future use. If you don't want to make a large amount of *miso-doko*, you can make a much smaller volume and apply it directly to the fish, curing it in a press-seal bag for the same amount of time. This is a useful technique if you're only cooking a small amount. If you don't have time for an overnight curing process, you can use the *miso-doko* as a marinade, marinating for at least an hour. The flavour will be much lighter than a proper curing process but it will still produce a nice meal. If you have time, however, I strongly recommend leaving the fish to cure for a day or two. The results are spectacular.

3 PREPARATION FOR GRILLING

It may be tempting to leave some of the miso clinging to the fish for additional flavour, but you should resist the temptation. Properly cured fish should be strongly flavoured enough, and any miso clinging to the outside of the fish is likely to burn and overwhelm the flavour of the fish. Don't rinse the fish under water, but scrape or wipe off as much of the miso as you can.

4 OTHER USES FOR THE *MISO-DOKO*

The *miso-doko* can be used for other ingredients. Chicken fillets are also delicious in this style, as is pork belly (see page 160). Vegetables can also be pickled in this mixture, and even raw egg yolk will cure to a glassy orange jelly that is delicious with hot rice. If you are curing raw foods that will not be cooked before eating (such as egg yolks), I recommend doing this before any raw meats or seafood have been added to the *miso-doko*. Kept in the fridge *miso-doko* like this can be used for around two weeks from the first round of curing, although you may need to season subsequent rounds of cured ingredients before adding them to the *miso-doko* as earlier ingredients absorb the salt. Just salt the ingredients lightly a few minutes before adding to the *miso-doko* and wipe away any moisture before adding.

NIZAKANA (soy-simmering)

煮魚

ALONG WITH SALT-GRILLING AND MISO-MARINATING, SOY-SIMMERING IS AMONG THE THREE
MOST POPULAR GENERAL STYLES OF PREPARING FISH IN JAPANESE CUISINE. IT IS WELL
SUITED TO AUTUMN AND WINTER COOKING.

INGREDIENTS

800g whole small to medium
   fish, scaled and cleaned,
   or around 400g fish fillets,
   scaled and cleaned (see
   Selection and Preparation)

SIMMERING LIQUID

½ cup Bonito Stock (page 30)
1 tsp sugar
2 tbsp mirin
2 tbsp sake
2 thin slices ginger, finely
   shredded (optional)
3 tbsp soy sauce

TO GARNISH

Small amount of greens, such
   as blanched snow pea or
   daikon shoots, green beans
   or okra

SELECTION AND PREPARATION

Nizakana literally means 'simmered fish', and it can be prepared
with many varieties of whole or filleted fish. Smaller or flatter
species are the most suitable as they can be simmered in a small
amount of liquid for greater control over the flavour of the fish.
Some good fish to prepare are: flounder, alfonsino, red emperor
(either fillets or whole fish), cod or dory. If simmering whole fish,
you may wish to score the flesh, similar to the pattern illustrated
for *shioyaki* (pages 123 and 124) to ensure even cooking. For fish
that are naturally slimy, pour boiling water over the fish first to stop
the slime from affecting the simmering liquid.

SIMMERING

Bring the Bonito Stock, sugar, mirin, sake and ginger to a simmer in a pot that just fits the fish in a single layer. Add the fish, skin side up, and baste with a few spoons of the stock. Reduce the heat to very low and cover with a drop lid or cartouche. Simmer for a few minutes, then add the soy sauce to the stock. (If you want the fish to be more strongly savoury, you can add the soy sauce earlier with the other simmering liquid ingredients.) Continue to simmer until the fish is cooked (this will depend on the size and type of the fish – dory fillets like those pictured will cook in about 8 minutes). Allow to cool slightly in the simmering liquid before serving. Transfer the fish to a warm serving plate and top with a few spoons of the liquid. Blanch any greens that you are using separately until just tender. Serve as a garnish for the fish.

1 PREPARING THE FISH
Most simmered dishes will include a two-stage cooking process. Ingredients are simmered in water first to remove some of the more harsh or raw flavours, and then transferred to a flavourful broth to absorb its seasoning and complete their cooking. Fish is no exception, but because it cooks so quickly a separate simmering process may result in overcooking. A quick rinse with boiling water may help remove any proteins or slime that might affect the flavour or texture of the simmering liquid.

2 SEASONINGS EXPLAINED

The simplicity of the seasonings for simmered fish are the key to its success. The stock adds umami and body to the simmering liquid. Soy sauce adds saltiness and umami. Mirin is used for sweetness and gloss, and to freshen the simmered flavour. Sake adds umami and the alcohol helps to carry flavour. More sake may be added for simmering river fish to mask any muddy aromas. The addition of ginger is for aromatic purposes, flavouring the dish but also helping to mask any fishy smells. You can also add aromatics such as yuzu citrus rind to simmering liquids like this.

3 THE IMPORTANCE OF DROP LIDS

Drop lids (or cartouches) play a very important role in all simmered dishes, and particularly with fish. They keep fish submerged within the simmering liquid and trap steam directly around the fish for more even cooking. They also allow evaporation around the edges where it will intensify the flavour without affecting the cooking of the fish. Lastly, their weight helps to hold delicate fish and other soft ingredients in place rather than letting them move in the convection currents of the simmering liquid. This prevents such delicate ingredients from breaking apart through the simmering process. For more on drop lids, see page 8.

4 SERVING

Simmered fish will benefit from a fresh garnish, such as a few fingers of blanched okra, snow peas or green beans. I prefer fish like this served warm on a warmed plate but it can also be served at room temperature or even chilled, where the stock will set to a jellied consistency. Fish prepared in this style will keep for a few days in the fridge, and its fishy flavours will intensify over time.

SNAPPER CHIRIMUSHI

鯛のちり蒸し

THIS DELICATE COLD WEATHER DISH PROVES THAT WINTER FOODS DON'T HAVE TO BE HEAVY
AND STODGY. IN JAPAN THIS IS MADE IN A LIDDED CERAMIC DISH, STEAMED WITH THE LID OFF
AND THEN COVERED FOR SERVING TO PRESERVE THE AROMA. THE CHIVES, AUTUMN-LEAF RADISH
AND PONZU AREN'T JUST GARNISHES – THEY ARE INTEGRAL TO THE SEASONING. YOU CAN USE
JUST ABOUT ANY WHITE FISH FILLETS FOR THIS, OR EVEN SALMON IF YOU PREFER.

INGREDIENTS

2 x 10cm square pieces of
    kombu (optional)
2 small snapper fillets (about
    120g each)
¼ tsp salt
300g silken tofu, pressed
    and cut into 2cm slices
2 thin slices lemon
2 shiitake mushrooms, stalks
    removed and caps reserved
100g shimeji mushrooms,
    broken into clumps
2 tsp sake
2 tbsp Autumn-leaf Radish
    (page 154)
2 tbsp finely chopped chives
3 tbsp Ponzu (page 102)

METHOD

1   Wipe the kombu with a dry cloth and place one piece in the
bottom of each bowl – you will need two heatproof bowls big
enough to hold half the ingredients. The bowls will be used both
for cooking and serving.

2   Season the snapper fillets with salt. Arrange one fillet in each
bowl along with half the tofu, a slice of lemon, a shiitake mushroom
and a small clump of shimeji mushrooms. Sprinkle with the sake
and steam the bowls for 10 minutes until the fish is cooked through.

3   Top the bowls with Autumn-leaf Radish and chopped chives,
and serve with the Ponzu alongside.

≫ If you're trying to decide whether a bowl you want to use for this dish
is suitable for putting into a steamer, I think a good rule of thumb is
whether you can put it in a dishwasher. A steamer will only reach 100°C
so most ceramic or glass dishes are fine to place inside them.

SERVES 2 **PREPARATION TIME** 30 MINS **COOKING TIME** 10 MINS

鯛も一人は
うまからず

Tai mo hitori ha umakarazu

Eaten alone, even sea bream loses its flavour.

The concept of *omotenashi* or hospitality is an important one for Japanese food. It recognises that far from being a solitary act, cooking and eating are some of the most communal things we do.

Most of the meals we eat in our lives will either be cooked for us by someone else, or otherwise be cooked by us to share with others. If you think of the favourite meals of your life, whether it's a cherished food from your childhood, a spectacular restaurant experience or just a great dish and a spirit of conviviality that snuck up and surprised you on a far-flung holiday, the one thing that most of the best food experiences have in common is that they are all usually shared experiences.

It is the nature of food to connect people.

I'm often asked why I love to cook, and this proverb goes a long way to explaining the way I feel about food. I have cooked for decades now, since I was a small boy. Cooking (and eating) for me has never been something I sought to do in isolation. Of course, there are days when I like nothing better than the quiet meditation of a day spent in the kitchen, but at the end of even the most solitary moments there has always been food to share.

I cook for my family every day and for that privilege I consider myself very lucky indeed. Anyone with kids will know that cooking for them is often a thankless task, but don't think of it just as one meal or one 'thank you'. Over months, years and decades it all becomes one great expression.

As an adult I now appreciate the thousands of meals my parents and grandparents made for me that resulted in books like this one, words like these and a set of principles around food that gets passed from one generation to another, one dinner at a time. I probably didn't thank them for every meal they made, but even if I had, that sentiment could never have captured everything it ultimately produced. One day I hope my kids will see things this way, too.

BARBARIAN SALMON

鮭の南蛮漬け

THE JAPANESE TERM FOR THIS STYLE OF MARINATING FRIED FOODS IN VINEGAR
IS *NANBANZUKE*, WHICH MEANS 'SOUTHERN BARBARIAN'. IT'S A TERM THAT WAS USED
TO REFER TO THE PORTUGUESE SAILORS WHO CAME TO JAPAN TO TRADE AROUND THE
16TH CENTURY AND INTRODUCED THEM TO DISHES LIKE ESCABECHE AND TEMPURA.
IT MAY NOT BE A POLITE TERM, BUT THE STYLE IS DELICIOUS.

INGREDIENTS

150ml Bonito Stock (page 30)
100ml rice vinegar
1 tbsp soy sauce
1 tsp sugar
1 small carrot, cut into fine
   matchsticks
2 thick spring onions, cut into
   fine matchsticks
1 stalk celery, cut into fine
   matchsticks
1 dried red chilli, cut into rings
500g salmon fillets, scaled and
   pinboned
2 tbsp potato starch or
   cornflour
About 2 cups oil, for shallow-
   frying

METHOD

1 Combine the stock, vinegar, soy sauce and sugar and stir to dissolve the sugar. Transfer the vinegar mixture to a deep tray and scatter with the vegetables and chilli.

2 Cut each salmon fillet into thirds lengthways. Dust the salmon pieces lightly in the potato starch, shaking off any excess.

3 Pour oil in a frying pan or saucepan to a depth of about 1cm and heat to 180°C. Fry the salmon pieces in batches for about 3 minutes each side until cooked through. Transfer each batch directly from the oil to the vinegar mixture as it cooks and place a few of the soaked vegetables on top of the salmon. The salmon pieces don't need to be completely submerged but it does help to turn them occasionally and you may want to prop up one side of the tray to collect the liquid at the other side. Marinate the salmon for at least 15 minutes and serve.

≫ This is also great as a preparation for chicken. Just cut the pieces quite small and shallow-fry them in a little more oil.

SERVES 4 **PREPARATION TIME** 20 MINS **COOKING TIME** 15 MINS, PLUS 15 MINS MARINATING TIME

SALMON ANKAKE

鮭のあんかけ

THE VEGETABLES THAT SMOTHER THIS SALMON DISH ARE PART DRESSING, PART
ACCOMPANIMENT AND PART SAUCE. JAPANESE FOOD DOESN'T ALWAYS FIT THE FORM
OF WESTERN COOKING, BUT I THINK THAT'S PART OF WHAT MAKES IT INTERESTING.

INGREDIENTS

2 small salmon fillets (150g
  each), skin removed
¼ cup cornflour
2 cups vegetable oil, for
  shallow-frying
2 cloves garlic, minced
1 small carrot, peeled and cut
  into batons
4 thick spring onions, sliced
  diagonally
1 tsp grated ginger
100g enoki mushrooms,
  trimmed and broken into
  clumps
2 spinach plants, washed and
  cut into 5cm lengths
2 cups All-purpose Chicken
  Dashi (page 31)
2 tbsp soy sauce
1 tbsp sake
1 tbsp rice vinegar
½ tsp sesame oil
½ tsp sugar
1 tbsp cornflour mixed with
  2 tbsp cold water
¼ tsp chilli oil (optional)

METHOD

1 Dust the salmon in cornflour and shake off any excess. Pour oil
into a wok or saucepan to a depth of about 2cm and heat to 180°C.
Shallow-fry the salmon for about 2 minutes each side until barely
cooked. Keep warm in a very low oven until ready to use.

2 In a separate saucepan, heat 2 tsp oil over high heat. Add the
garlic, carrot and spring onion and fry for about 2 minutes until
starting to soften. Add the ginger, mushrooms and spinach, and stir
for another minute. Add the dashi, soy sauce, sake, rice vinegar,
sesame oil and sugar, and bring to a simmer. Simmer for 5 minutes,
then add the cornflour mixture in a thin stream while stirring.
Simmer for a further minute until the sauce thickens to a silky
consistency.

3 Place each salmon fillet onto a serving dish and spoon the
vegetables and sauce over the top. Finish with a few drops of chilli
oil if using.

≫ The key with this dish is to get the sauce just right. Well-balanced,
slightly sour and silky without being too thin or too thick.

SERVES 2 **PREPARATION TIME** 20 MINS **COOKING TIME** 20 MINS

一尺の薪を
くべるより
一寸の
蓋をしろ

Issyaku no maki o kuberuyori issun no futa o shiro
Instead of adding firewood, put a lid on for a second.

For simmered dishes, the control of heat is important, but the use of drop lids (*otoshibuta*) is even more vital. Where controlling heat affects only the intensity of cooking, the lid controls both the heat and the seasoning. Adding a drop lid will keep steam around simmering ingredients, gently cooking them, while still allowing evaporation of the simmering liquid. As the liquid evaporates, its seasoning intensifies, which is vital to the success of such dishes.

For dishes like the Kingfish and Daikon (page 144) and Braised Tuna (page 147) that follow, or for the many other braised and simmered dishes in other parts of this book, the goal is to achieve well-cooked ingredients that have been infused with the flavour of the broth, together with a small amount of appropriately reduced broth used almost like a loose dressing.

I've tried to help you as best I can with the recipes in this book tested on multiple different stoves, but with variables in pot size, flame strength and quality of ingredients, much will depend on your own intuition as a cook. If your simmered dishes lack flavour, instead of needing to add more seasonings perhaps it is just that not enough liquid has evaporated in the cooking process. If those dishes are too dry and strong, it may be that too much of the broth has evaporated away.

Achieving a marriage between an agreeable texture of cooked ingredients and a good flavour from absorbed seasonings may be a little tricky at first, but it will soon become second nature. Every Japanese cook must learn this at some stage.

KINGFISH AND DAIKON

ブリ大根

BURI, A SPECIES OF YELLOWTAIL, IS ONE OF JAPAN'S FAVOURITE WINTER FISH, AND THIS DISH IS IN EVERY HOME COOK'S REPERTOIRE. IT'S LIGHT AND EASY TO MAKE, BUT ALSO FLAVOURFUL AND COMFORTING. IT'S THE KIND OF DISH WHERE THE NUANCES OF MAKING IT GET PASSED DOWN WITHIN A FAMILY FROM GENERATION TO GENERATION. WHERE A GRANDCHILD WILL LEARN TO MAKE IT EXACTLY THE SAME WAY THEIR GRANDPARENTS DID. IN AUSTRALIA, KINGFISH IS A PERFECT SUBSTITUTE.

INGREDIENTS

750g kingfish fillets (or other
  firm-fleshed white fish)
½ large daikon
¼ cup soy sauce
5 tbsp sake
2 tbsp mirin
2 tbsp sugar
2cm ginger, peeled and cut into
  fine matchsticks, to serve

METHOD

1   Clean the kingfish and cut into 5cm pieces. Peel the daikon and cut into 2cm rounds. Bevel the edges of the daikon to create a rounded puck shape.

2   Place the daikon into a large saucepan and cover with cold water. Bring to a simmer and simmer for about 25 minutes until the daikon is tender. Add the soy sauce, sake, mirin and sugar, and simmer for a further 10 minutes, covered with a drop lid or foil cartouche if it starts to get too dry. Add the kingfish and simmer for about 6 minutes, uncovered, until the fish is just cooked and the liquid is reduced. Allow to cool slightly and serve garnished with the ginger.

≫ Bevelling the edges of the daikon stops it from breaking and keeps the simmering liquid clear. Once you get the technique right, it only takes a few seconds and it is very worthwhile doing.

SERVES 4   **PREPARATION TIME** 15 MINS   **COOKING TIME** 45 MINS

BRAISED TUNA

マグロの角煮

BRAISED DISHES IN THIS STYLE ARE USUALLY MADE WITH MEATS
LIKE PORK BELLY, BUT USING TUNA GIVES IT A MUCH LIGHTER
TEXTURE WITHOUT COMPROMISING ITS RICH, SAVOURY FLAVOUR.

INGREDIENTS

⅓ cup soy sauce
⅓ cup mirin
⅓ cup sake
⅓ cup Bonito Stock (page 30)
 or water
1 tbsp sugar
2cm ginger, peeled and thinly
 sliced
600g raw tuna steaks, cut into
 5cm pieces

METHOD

1 Place the liquid ingredients, sugar and ginger in a large saucepan and bring to a simmer. Simmer for 5–10 minutes until the mixture starts to thicken and reduce. Add the tuna, cover with a drop lid or cartouche and simmer again for 5 minutes.

2 Remove the drop lid, stir the tuna and simmer, uncovered, for a further 2–3 minutes, until the sauce is thickened and reduced in the bottom of the saucepan. Allow to cool to room temperature and serve.

≫ Like many Japanese dishes, this can be served warm, at room temperature or even chilled. If serving warm, still allow the tuna to cool in the braising liquid then gently reheat to serve.

SERVES 4 **PREPARATION TIME** 5 MINS **COOKING TIME** 15 MINS

chapter
seven meat

From the 7th century until the late 19th century, eating meat in Japan was stigmatised and for much of that time banned at least partially by law (with varying degrees of strictness). The hand-wringing lawmakers of the time, inspired by Buddhist teaching, sought to outlaw certain foods. Historical records indicate that while these bans were in place for more than a thousand years, they were barely observed by the people.

The punchline is that Japan now produces some of the best meat and poultry in the world, and yet the magnificent quality of wagyu beef, kurobuta pork and cochin chickens might not have been possible without the ill-advised meat bans of the last millennium.

Quality over quantity is the mantra. Meat is certainly popular in Japan these days, but the cultural hangover of centuries of presumptive taboo has meant that it is still viewed as somewhat of an indulgence. Meat tends to be eaten in smaller amounts of much higher quality, an approach that is better for taste, better for the environment and better for health. While I don't advocate banning yourself from eating meat for a thousand years to get to this point, what has evolved from this quirk of history is a very sensible way of eating indeed.

STEAMED PORK WITH SESAME SAUCE

蒸し豚の胡麻だれ

I THINK WHAT FIRST DREW ME TO COOKING JAPANESE FOOD REGULARLY AT HOME WAS ITS SIMPLICITY. ANYONE CAN MAKE A JAPANESE DISH FOR A SPECIAL OCCASION OR A DINNER PARTY, BUT UNLESS A DISH IS QUICK, EASY AND DELICIOUS, IT WON'T BE TURNING UP ON AN ORDINARY WEEKNIGHT DINNER TABLE. JAPANESE CUISINE IS FULL OF DISHES LIKE THAT, AND THIS IS ONE OF THEM.

INGREDIENTS

500g pork belly, skin and
  bones removed, cut into
  5cm wide strips
1 tsp salt
3 cups cabbage, very finely
  shredded
½ cup Sesame Sauce
  (page 103)
4 thin spring onions, finely
  sliced

METHOD

1 Place a bamboo steamer over a large saucepan or wok of boiling water. Season the pork well with the salt and place into the steamer. Cover and steam for 20–25 minutes then remove from the heat. Alternatively, cook in a steam oven set on full steam for the same amount of time. Rest for about 10 minutes in a warm place then slice crossways into 1cm slices.

2 Arrange the cabbage onto a serving plate to form a base and place the pork slices on top. Dress with the Sesame Sauce and scatter over the spring onions.

≫ Shred the cabbage on a large mandoline if you have one (Benriner is the most popular Japanese brand), but otherwise you can do it by hand with a sharp knife and a bit of patience.

SERVES 4 **PREPARATION TIME** 15 MINS **COOKING TIME** 20 MINS

CHICKEN AND PRAWN CHAWANMUSHI

茶碗蒸し

THESE SAVOURY CUSTARDS LOOK IMPRESSIVE BUT ARE EASY TO MAKE. JUST ARRANGE YOUR INGREDIENTS IN A SMALL HEATPROOF BOWL AND POUR OVER THE CUSTARD MIX. THE RATIO OF EGGS TO STOCK SHOULD BE AROUND 1:3 FOR A VERY DELICATE, BARELY SET CUSTARD. IF YOU PREFER YOUR CUSTARD TO BE A LITTLE MORE SOLID, YOU CAN DECREASE THE AMOUNT OF STOCK.

INGREDIENTS

100g chicken breast fillet or tenderloin, cut into thin slices
4 raw prawns, peeled
2 fresh shiitake mushrooms, stems removed and caps thinly sliced
1 tsp sake
Pinch of salt
4 chives, cut into 5cm lengths, to serve

EGG CUSTARD BASE

3 large eggs (to yield ½ cup of beaten egg)
1½ cups Bonito Stock (page 30) or All-purpose Chicken Dashi (page 31)
1 tsp mirin
1 tsp soy sauce
¼ tsp salt

METHOD

1 First, make the custard base. Beat the eggs slowly, taking care not to incorporate too much air into the eggs, and mix with the remaining custard ingredients to a smooth liquid.

2 Toss the chicken, prawn and shiitake mushrooms with the sake and salt, and arrange in two small heatproof bowls. Pour the custard through a sieve over the ingredients and tap the bowls a few times to bring any bubbles to the surface. Pop the bubbles with a skewer or a very quick blow with a blowtorch. Place into a hot steamer. Immediately reduce the heat to very low and steam for 10 minutes. Alternatively, cook in a steam oven on full steam. Turn off the heat, or remove from the steam oven, and allow to stand for a further 2 minutes. Garnish with the chives and serve.

≫ Don't add too many ingredients to the bowl, as they will release liquid as they cook, affecting the consistency of the custard. Also try to avoid liquid from the steamer dripping into the bowls. A bamboo steamer lid should prevent this, but if you find your steamer is letting drips ruin your custard, you can cover the individual custards with aluminium foil and just steam them for a little longer.

SERVES 2 **PREPARATION TIME** 15 MINS **COOKING TIME** 15 MINS

WAGYU WITH AUTUMN-LEAF RADISH

和牛ステーキのもみじおろし添え

GOOD-QUALITY JAPANESE BEEF (WAGYU) IS HEAVILY MARBLED AND QUITE RICH, SO IT'S BETTER TO SHARE IT. THIS DISH IS HOW I APPROACH EATING MEAT – PICK THE BEST QUALITY MEAT YOU CAN, COOK IT WELL, SERVE IT SIMPLY AND SHARE IT.

INGREDIENTS

½ tsp vegetable oil
1 wagyu sirloin steak (about 250g)
1 tsp salt
Lemon wedge, to serve
1 tsp Boosted Soy Sauce (page 28), to serve

AUTUMN-LEAF RADISH

1 red bird's-eye chilli
Block of peeled daikon (about 5cm square and 8cm long)

METHOD

1 To make the Autumn-leaf Radish, cut the stalk from the chilli and remove the seeds from the centre with a skewer. Using a pointed chopstick, poke a hole into the daikon block a little longer than the chilli. Place the chilli over the end of the chopstick and push it into the hole. Alternatively, you can cut a slit into the end of the daikon and push a sliver of chilli inside. Grate the daikon block with a fine Japanese grater or rasp grater, pushing the chilli side directly onto the grater. Transfer the grated daikon to a fine sieve and allow to stand for 5 minutes to drain off any excess moisture released by the daikon.

2 Heat a heavy-based frying pan over high heat and coat the base with a little vegetable oil. Season the steak well with salt and fry to medium rare. Rest well, and slice into thick slices.

3 Place the sliced steak onto a warmed plate with a small pile of the Autumn-leaf Radish and a wedge of lemon. Serve with the Boosted Soy Sauce.

≫ The lightly spicy 'autumn-leaf radish' (*momiji-oroshi*) is named because its colour resembles that of Japanese maple leaves in autumn. A little pile of wasabi is a great substitute if you don't want to go to the effort of making it.

SERVES 2 **PREPARATION TIME** 10 MINS **COOKING TIME** 10 MINS

食べて
すぐ寝ると
牛になる

Tabete suguneru to ushi ni naru

Sleep soon after eating and you'll turn into a cow.

It's a warning that Japanese parents have been telling their kids for hundreds of years. Retiring to bed soon after a meal will make you as fat and lazy as cattle.

The sumo wrestlers of Japan attribute their gigantic size not to unhealthy food – their staple dish is Chanko Nabe, a light and nutritious stew not dissimilar to Shabu-shabu (page 90) or Soy Milk Nabe (page 94) – but to their training habit of napping straight after a big meal, a technique specifically employed to help build their formidable heft.

It's incredible to me just how accurate many of the old wisdoms are. It may today seem obvious with the benefit of hindsight and all the scientific knowledge of the history of the world just a few keystrokes away, but these messages for health came before calorie counting and glycaemic indices, before we understood about blood sugar and how even just a little physical activity after a meal can avoid spikes and crashes.

It may seem like just a throwaway comment that a parent uses just to get a child to do as they're told, but in truth this is information paid for by lifetimes of observation, and shared from generation to generation.

CHICKEN NEGISHIO

鶏のネギ塩焼き

CHICKEN HAS A BAD REPUTATION IN MANY WESTERN COUNTRIES AS BEING BLAND, BUT IN JAPAN THERE IS NONE OF THAT. IT'S CONFUSING, REALLY. HOW CAN WE KNOW THAT CHICKEN STOCK IS A FABULOUS SOURCE OF FLAVOUR BUT STILL BELIEVE THAT CHICKEN MEAT IS TASTELESS?

The problem is that in the West we're terrified of raw chicken and consequently overcook it, forcing out all of the delicious juices. In Japan, chicken is eaten every way, from well-done to very rare and even raw! Even if you can't stand the idea of medium-rare chicken, just make sure you don't overcook it. Well-cooked chicken should be juicy and flavourful no matter how done it is.

INGREDIENTS

1 tbsp vegetable oil
500g chicken thighs, skin on
½ tsp salt flakes
½ cup thin spring onions, finely chopped
1 tsp sesame oil
½ tsp sesame seeds, to serve
Lemon wedges, to serve

METHOD

1 Heat a heavy frying pan over high heat and add the oil. Season the chicken well with half the salt and fry the chicken, skin side down first, until brown and crisp, about 3 minutes. Then turn and fry until barely cooked through, about another 2 minutes. You may wish to turn the chicken a few times while frying to brown it evenly. Allow to rest for a few minutes and cut into thick slices.

2 Toss the spring onion, sesame oil, sesame seeds and remaining salt together, and scatter on top of the chicken. Serve with lemon wedges.

≫ This dish hinges on the simplicity and accuracy of its seasoning. *Negishio* means 'onion and salt' and you really need to have the correct amount of salt to bring the onion and chicken together. This is also delicious with strips of pan-fried pork belly.

SERVES 4 **PREPARATION TIME** 10 MINS **COOKING TIME** 10 MINS

MISO-CURED PORK

豚バラの味噌漬け

I TEND TO MAKE THIS DISH WITH ANY LEFTOVER MISO MIXTURE USED FOR CURING FISH OR
VEGETABLES EARLIER IN THE WEEK. THE RESULT IS A STRONGLY FLAVOURED MEATY DISH THAT'S
A LITTLE LIKE THICK-CUT JAPANESE BACON. YOU DON'T NEED A LOT OF IT TO SATISFY YOU.

INGREDIENTS

100g white miso
1 tbsp mirin
1kg pork belly, skin and bones
   removed and cut into 7cm
   wide strips
¼ tsp salt
1 tsp vegetable oil

METHOD

1 Mix the miso and mirin together to a smooth paste. Rub the
pork belly in salt first, and then coat in the miso mixture. Cover
with plastic wrap or place into a press-seal bag and refrigerate
for at least 24 hours.

2 Heat your oven to 180°C. Remove the pork from the miso
mixture, scrape off any excess miso with a butter knife then wipe
with a bit of kitchen paper to remove as much miso as possible.
Rub the pork all over with the vegetable oil. Place the pork on a
lightly oiled rack on a baking tray to catch drips and roast in the
oven for about 20–25 minutes until darkly roasted and cooked
through. Rest for 5 minutes, then slice and serve.

≫ This dish is fine just as it is, but if you are looking for a way to
present it nicely to serve, you could do worse than a mound of finely
shaved cabbage and a big dollop of Japanese mayonnaise sprinkled
with shichimi togarashi.

SERVES 4–6 **PREPARATION TIME** 10 MINS, PLUS OVERNIGHT CURING **COOKING TIME** 25 MINS + 5 MINS RESTING

TERIYAKI PORK AND MUSHROOM ROLLS

えのきの豚巻

THERE ARE SO MANY DIFFERENT WAYS TO USE YOUR TERIYAKI GLAZE (PAGE 28) BEYOND
JUST CHICKEN, BEEF OR FISH. IT REALLY IS ONE OF THE MOST USEFUL THINGS IN MY PANTRY.
YOU'LL NEED VERY THINLY SLICED PORK FOR THIS. TAKE A LOOK AT THE BUTASHABU SALAD
(PAGE 106) FOR A FEW SUGGESTIONS ON WHERE TO FIND SOME.

INGREDIENTS

200g enoki mushrooms
300g skinless pork belly, or
    bacon, very thinly sliced
2 tbsp vegetable oil
3 cherry tomatoes, for garnish
¼ cup Teriyaki Glaze (page 28)

METHOD

1 Trim the dirty ends from the mushrooms and break them into
thick clumps about 1cm in diameter. Wrap each clump with a strip
or two of pork belly.

2 Heat a frying pan over medium-high heat and add the vegetable
oil. Fry the whole cherry tomatoes until the skin starts to wrinkle
and blacken, then remove from the pan and set aside. Add the
rolls to the pan and fry for about 3 minutes until the pork is well-
browned. Add the Teriyaki Glaze and cover for 3 minutes to allow
the pork and mushrooms to steam, then remove the cover and roll
the rolls through the glaze as it thickens to coat them. Remove from
the heat and serve the rolls garnished with the tomatoes.

≫ If using bacon or thicker slices of pork belly for this dish, you may need
to secure the rolls with a toothpick or skewer, as the thicker the pork is,
the less the rolls will hold together.

SERVES 2–4 **PREPARATION TIME** 10 MINS **COOKING TIME** 10 MINS

CHICKEN AND TOFU MEATBALLS

豆腐入り鶏つくね

THE REASON WE SOMETIMES ADD 'FILLERS' TO MEATBALLS AND HAMBURGERS
IS NOT TO BIND THE MEAT TOGETHER, AS SOME WOULD BELIEVE, BUT TO CREATE
A SOFTER TEXTURE. WHILE MOST USE BREADCRUMBS, TOFU IS AN EVEN BETTER
FILLER AS IT HOLDS MOISTURE FOR A JUICIER RESULT.

INGREDIENTS

300g firm tofu, drained
500g chicken mince
1 onion, coarsely grated
1 egg
½ tsp salt
1 tbsp vegetable oil
½ cup Teriyaki Glaze (page 28)
3 green oak-leaf lettuce leaves,
   to serve
½ tsp mixed black and golden
   sesame seeds, toasted
1 tbsp Japanese mayonnaise,
   to serve

METHOD

1 Drain the tofu and press between two plates for about 15 minutes to remove excess moisture. Crumble the tofu into a large bowl and mix through the mince, onion, egg and salt. Form into patty-shaped meatballs about 8cm long, 5cm wide, and 5cm thick. Refrigerate for about 20 minutes to allow the meatballs to firm.

2 Heat the oil in a large frying pan over medium heat and fry the meatballs in batches, turning often, for about 6 minutes until cooked through. After the last batch is cooked, return all the meatballs to the pan and add the Teriyaki Glaze. Turn the meatballs regularly through the glaze as it thickens to coat them.

3 Arrange the lettuce leaves on a plate and place the meatballs on top. Scatter with the sesame seeds and serve with a dollop of mayonnaise.

≫ You could make these into larger hamburger-sized patties if you prefer. They will just take a little longer to cook.

SERVES 4 **PREPARATION TIME** 20 MINS, PLUS 20 MINS RESTING TIME **COOKING TIME** 15 MINS

CHIKUZEN-NI

筑前煮

THIS SPECIALTY FROM THE CHIKUZEN PROVINCE IN FUKUOKA PREFECTURE IS A BRILLIANT EXAMPLE OF HOW JAPANESE CUISINE PRESERVES THE FLAVOUR OF INDIVIDUAL INGREDIENTS. EACH ELEMENT OF THIS FRIED-THEN-BRAISED DISH IS SEASONED WITH A STRONG BRAISING LIQUID AND IS INTENSELY FLAVOURED, BUT STILL RETAINS ITS UNIQUE FLAVOUR. CHICKEN TASTES LIKE CHICKEN, MUSHROOMS TASTE LIKE MUSHROOM, AND THE SNOW PEAS AT THE END LIGHTEN THE BRAISED ELEMENTS, CREATING TEXTURE AND VARIETY.

INGREDIENTS

5 dried shiitake mushrooms
1 small burdock root (optional)
1 small carrot
1 small lotus root
150g konnyaku jelly (optional)
1 tbsp sesame oil
450g chicken thigh fillets, cut into 5cm pieces
2 tbsp sugar
2 tbsp sake
2 tbsp mirin
2 tbsp soy sauce
10 snow peas, blanched and halved on an angle

METHOD

1 Rinse the shiitake mushrooms quickly in cold water and then soak in 2 cups of hot water until softened. Remove stems and reserve the soaking liquid. If using burdock, scrape with the back of a knife under running water to remove any hair-like roots or woody blemishes; don't remove all of the skin as this has the most flavour. Cut the burdock, carrot and lotus root into chunks.

2 Place the konnyaku in cold water in a small saucepan. Bring to a rolling boil and boil for 5 minutes. Drain and cut into large pieces.

3 Heat the sesame oil and fry the root vegetables (carrot, lotus root, burdock). Add the konnyaku and chicken, and fry for about a minute. Add 1 cup shiitake liquid and the sugar, sake, mirin and soy sauce. Simmer, covered with a drop lid, for about 10 minutes. Remove the lid, stir and simmer, uncovered, for a further 5 minutes until nearly dry. Allow to cool to room temperature and either serve at room temperature or reheat it to serve.

4 Transfer the ingredients to a presentation dish, arranging the elements attractively, then add the snow peas throughout the dish and serve.

≫ If you can't find unusual ingredients such as burdock and konnyaku (they are sold in Japanese grocery stores), don't worry about substituting something else. Just leave them out.

SERVES 4–6 **PREPARATION TIME** 25 MINS **COOKING TIME** 25 MINS

chapter
eight

mainly
vegetables

I'm no vegetarian but it's always struck me that a meat-focused diet misses a very real opportunity. We have thousands of varieties of fish and hundreds of varieties of vegetables to choose from, and yet we most often plan our meals around one of four or five different meats.

The exquisite variety of Japanese food comes from the fact that vegetables are treated not as side dishes or accompaniments to meat or even fish, but as ingredients worthy of our attention in their own right. As with all things, the goal is just to present a vegetable's flavour simply and faithfully. It can be as basic as a beautiful Hokkaido potato steamed slowly for an hour to intensify its natural sweetness, or even an exquisite tomato simply sliced and served with a little salt (page 173) that tastes so good it makes you wonder why nobody thought of it sooner.

SALTED CABBAGE

塩キャベツ

THIS SALTED CABBAGE IS A POPULAR DISH TO SERVE ALONGSIDE GRILLED CHICKEN SKEWERS (*YAKITORI*). IT'S EATEN ALMOST AS A PALATE CLEANSER, WITH THE FRESHNESS OF THE CABBAGE WORKING AS A COUNTERPOINT TO THE SMOKY CHAR OF THE SKEWERS.

INGREDIENTS

½ small head cabbage
½ tsp salt
1 tsp sesame oil
¼ tsp sesame seeds

METHOD

1 Cut the cabbage into large pieces and sprinkle with salt. Allow to stand for 5 minutes, then rinse well in very cold water. Place in the fridge until ready to serve. Spin in a salad spinner and place into a large bowl.

2 Sprinkle with the sesame oil and sesame seeds to serve.

≫ Keep the cabbage well chilled so that it retains its crispness. This is a great side dish for a barbecue.

SERVES 4–8, AS A SIDE DISH **PREPARATION TIME** 10 MINS **COOKING TIME** 0 MINS

HIYASHI TOMATO

冷やしトマト

I'LL ALWAYS REMEMBER THE FIRST TIME I HAD THIS DISH – AND IT'S BARELY EVEN
A DISH, REALLY. JUST A CHILLED TOMATO THAT BRINGS OUT THE BEST OF BOTH TEXTURE
AND FLAVOUR. I SAW IT ON A MENU AT A TINY LOCAL RESTAURANT NEAR MY APARTMENT
IN TOKYO AND SCOFFED AT IT. A SINGLE TOMATO FOR $4? BUT AFTER I HAD IT, I WAS
CONVINCED IT WAS ONE OF THE BEST TOMATO DISHES I'VE EVER HAD. THE PERFECT TASTE
OF A TOMATO, UNCLUTTERED AND UNADULTERATED. SOMETIMES ALL YOU HAVE TO DO
TO BE A GREAT COOK IS JUST GET OUT OF THE WAY.

INGREDIENTS

¼ tsp salt flakes or powdered
salt
1 very, very good quality
tomato
1 shiso leaf, for garnish

METHOD

1   If using salt flakes, grind in a mortar until it becomes a fine
powder.

2   Fill a large bowl with ice and water to create a slurry. Plunge
the tomato into the water for 30 seconds, then remove it, slice it
into 1cm slices or thick wedges and serve on a shiso leaf with the
powdered salt on the side.

≫ You should never keep tomatoes in the fridge as the cold denatures
the flavour-producing enzymes in the fruit. This dish chills the outside
for texture while inside the enzymes are still able to produce rich
tomato flavour.

SMALL DISH **PREPARATION TIME** 1 MIN **COOKING TIME** 0 MINS

QUICK SOY-STEEPED SPINACH

ほうれん草のおひたし

IF THERE IS A SINGLE DISH FROM THIS BOOK THAT MAKES THE MOST REGULAR APPEARANCE ON OUR DINING TABLE, IT'S THIS ONE. WE WILL OFTEN COOK A BUNCH OF SPINACH EARLY IN THE WEEK AND JUST LEAVE IT IN THE FRIDGE. WE HAVE BOOSTED SOY SAUCE ALWAYS TO HAND AND THE BONITO FLAKES LIVE IN THE PANTRY. FROM THAT STARTING POINT, IF WE NEED AN EXTRA DISH FOR THE TABLE, THIS CAN BE READY IN LESS THAN A MINUTE.

INGREDIENTS

1 bunch spinach, washed and soaked in a sink or large bowl of cold water for at least 10 minutes
1 tbsp Boosted Soy Sauce (page 28)
1 tsp bonito flakes

METHOD

1 Bring a large saucepan of water to a rolling boil. Place the root and stems of the spinach into the water and hold for about 10 seconds. Then, using a pair of chopsticks, push the leaves under water and cook for about 1 minute. Drain and rinse in cold water. You can keep the spinach whole in the fridge, soaking in a bowl of cold water, for up to a week.

2 When ready to eat, remove the spinach from the water and squeeze out as much liquid as possible. Cut off and discard the roots, and trim the stalks and leaves into 5cm pieces. Stack the pieces in a bowl, pour over a little Boosted Soy Sauce and scatter with bonito flakes.

≫ Soaking the spinach in cold water before cooking allows it to refresh and open up, like a bunch of flowers might, allowing any dirt between the stalks to wash out into the water.

SMALL DISH **PREPARATION TIME** 5 MINS **COOKING TIME** 5 MINS

SOY-FLAVOURED EGGS

味玉

YOU'VE PROBABLY SEEN THESE EGGS IN A BOWL OF RAMEN BEFORE, BUT THEY
CAN BE USED FOR SO MUCH MORE. TRY THEM AS A DISH ON THEIR OWN, OR ADD
THEM TO A DONBURI, NOODLE DISH OR SALAD.

INGREDIENTS

6 extra-large eggs
1 cup Boosted Soy Sauce
  (page 28)
½ cup Bonito Stock (page 30)
1 clove garlic, sliced

METHOD

1 Bring a large saucepan of water to a rolling boil. With a pin, prick a hole in the round end of each egg. Place all the eggs into a sieve and dip into the boiling water two or three times to acclimatise the eggs so that they don't crack.

2 Place the eggs into the water and stir the water and eggs gently for 1 minute to centre the yolks within the whites, then boil for a further 6 minutes (total 7 minutes). Remove the eggs from the water and immediately plunge into a bowl of cold water placed in the sink. Run more cold water over the eggs for a few minutes until they are cool to the touch.

3 Peel the eggs in the bowl of water and transfer to a plastic container. Combine the soy sauce, stock and garlic and pour over the eggs, ensuring they are completely covered. You may need to place a drop lid or plate on top of the eggs to keep them covered. Depending on the size and shape of your container, you may need to adjust the amount of steeping liquid to ensure the eggs are fully submerged. Refrigerate for 8–12 hours, gently stirring the eggs every few hours to make sure they are well coated. Halve the eggs to serve.

≫ You can adjust the flavour of the eggs by the concentration of soy sauce to stock, and the amount of time the eggs steep in the liquid. I prefer my eggs quite strongly flavoured, and that's what you'll get from this recipe. If they're too much for you, try increasing the amount of stock and/or decreasing the steeping time.

MAKES 6 EGGS **PREPARATION TIME** 5 MINS **COOKING TIME** 7 MINS, PLUS 12 HOURS STEEPING

CUCUMBER AND WAKAME

きゅうりとわかめの酢の物

VINEGAR-DRESSED DISHES LIKE THIS ONE TAKE JUST A FEW MINUTES TO MAKE,
BUT CAN PROVIDE IMPORTANT BALANCE TO OILY FISH OR SAVOURY SIMMERED DISHES.

INGREDIENTS

5g dried wakame
1 Lebanese cucumber, very
   thinly sliced into rounds
3 tsp rice vinegar
2 tsp sugar
1 tsp soy sauce

≫ The sanbaizu (literally, three
scoop vinegar) is a very popular
sauce for simply poached seafood
or as a dressing for vinegared
dishes like this.

METHOD

1   Rinse the wakame in tap water and place in a heatproof bowl,
covering with additional tap water and allowing to stand for around
10 minutes. Drain the water, then pour boiling water over the
wakame and allow to stand for a minute or so until softened. Plunge
into a bowl of iced water, drain and cut into 2cm lengths.

2   Toss the wakame and cucumber together. Mix the vinegar, sugar
and soy together (this is called sanbaizu) and stir to dissolve the
sugar. Liberally dress the wakame and cucumber and serve.

SERVES 4 AS A SIDE DISH   **PREPARATION TIME** 15 MINS   **COOKING TIME** 0 MINS

BITTER GOURD OHITASHI

ゴーヤのおひたし

THE SHORT BLANCHING IN BOILING WATER IS NOT INTENDED TO COOK
THE GOURD, BUT TO SOFTEN IT AND REMOVE SOME OF THE SHARP BITTERNESS.

INGREDIENTS

½ bitter gourd
¼ tsp salt
½ tsp sesame oil
¼ tsp Boosted Soy Sauce
   (page 28)
1 tsp bonito flakes

≫ In putting together a Japanese
meal, small dishes like this provide
important variety and contrast.

METHOD

1   To prepare the bitter gourd, cut it in half lengthways and scoop
out the seeds and spongy white pith with a spoon. Slice thinly and
scatter with the salt. Allow to stand for 15 minutes.

2   Bring a small saucepan of water to a rolling boil and add the bitter
gourd. Blanch for 20 seconds then transfer to a bowl of iced water.

3   Drain well, squeezing out as much water as possible, then dress
with the sesame oil and Boosted Soy Sauce and scatter with bonito
flakes.

SMALL DISH   **PREPARATION TIME** 10 MINS, PLUS 15 MINUTES STANDING   **COOKING TIME** 1 MIN

COLD CUCUMBERS WITH SNAPPER MISO

きゅうりと鯛味噌

CUCUMBERS ARE THE FLAVOUR OF JAPANESE SUMMER. THEY'RE SERVED ON STICKS
CHILLED IN ICE AT SUMMER FESTIVALS AND EVERY JAPANESE CHILD WILL HAVE FOND
MEMORIES OF THE CRISP AND REFRESHING SNAP OF AN ICE-COLD CUCUMBER AGAINST
THE HUMID SUMMER HEAT. IT BEATS FAIRY FLOSS, THAT'S FOR SURE.

INGREDIENTS

2 Japanese, Korean or
   Lebanese cucumbers, chilled
Crushed ice, to serve

SNAPPER MISO (makes extra)
1 snapper head (about 300g),
   or other offcuts, or 1 small
   snapper fillet (about 150g)
500ml No. 1 Stock (page 30),
   or water
2 tbsp sake
1 cup brown miso

METHOD

1 To make the snapper miso, place the snapper head in a
medium saucepan with the stock and sake. Bring to a simmer
and simmer for about 30 minutes. Remove the head, allow to cool
slightly and pick off all the meat, discarding the skin and bones.

2 Transfer the meat to a mortar and grind to a paste. Add the
miso and continue to grind until a smooth paste forms. Transfer to
an airtight container. The snapper miso will keep in the fridge for
about three weeks.

3 Peel the cucumber in intervals and cut into long, thick batons
the same length as the cucumber. Serve the batons of cucumber
on crushed ice with a little of the snapper miso on the side.

≫ This dip is a great way of using up leftover snapper. Alternatively, skip
the snapper altogether and just use a good-quality miso for dipping. You
can get looser styles of miso, known as *moromi* miso, that are made
specifically for dipping.

SERVES 4 AS PART OF A SHARED MEAL **PREPARATION TIME** 10 MINS **COOKING TIME** 40 MINS

EGGPLANT WITH CAPSICUM AND MISO

ナスとピーマンの鍋しぎ

STIR-FRYING ISN'T TRADITIONAL TO JAPANESE CUISINE, BUT IT'S BECOMING INCREASINGLY POPULAR IN JAPANESE HOMES. IT CAN BE USED FOR NEW DISHES, OR TO BRING NEW LIFE TO CLASSIC DISHES. THIS *NABESHIGE* DISH IS TRADITIONALLY MADE IN A SAUCEPAN, BUT I THINK USING A WOK PRODUCES EVEN BETTER RESULTS.

INGREDIENTS

2 tbsp sesame oil

1 medium eggplant, cut into rolling chunks

1 small green capsicum, cut into rolling chunks

1 small dried red chilli, seeds removed and sliced into rounds

1 tbsp sake

2 tbsp mirin

1 tbsp soy sauce

½ tbsp sugar

1 tbsp red miso

1 tbsp Bonito Stock (page 30) or water

METHOD

1   Heat the sesame oil in a wok or medium frying pan over medium-high heat and fry the eggplant and capsicum until lightly browned. Add the chilli, sake, mirin, soy sauce and sugar, toss for a minute then cover with a lid. Simmer for 2 minutes, then remove the lid and stir through the miso mixed with the stock. Continue to toss for a further few minutes until the liquid has reduced to a thick glaze and the vegetables are cooked through.

≫ Miso is a perfect ready-made stir-fry seasoning. Just mix it with a little liquid and add it to your favourite stir-fry ingredients.

SERVES 4 AS PART OF A SHARED MEAL   **PREPARATION TIME** 15 MINS   **COOKING TIME** 15 MINS

三里四方の野菜を食べろ

Sanri shihou no yasai o tabero

Eat vegetables from within 3-li.

Eating locally is a popular concept these days, a reaction to the fact that what ends up on our tables can sometimes come from every corner of the globe, with little regard for the consequences.

This old idiom asks us to eat vegetables grown within 3-li of where we are, an archaic measurement of length roughly equivalent to about 12 kilometres. Our idea of eating locally is informed by a desire to eat seasonally or to reduce the environmental impact of our food, but idioms like this had very little to do with food miles or carbon footprint in the days before ocean freighters and jumbo jets.

Local eating is more about community and a connection to a place than it is about saving the planet. In earlier times, eating vegetables from within 3-li meant supporting your neighbours, and understanding more about what it means to produce the food we eat. If you've ever grown a vegetable yourself, and experienced just how much more care and effort you take when cooking and eating it compared to something you've just picked up from the shops, you'll know exactly what I mean.

Our concept of locality or place has expanded beyond a 12-kilometre radius these days, but what has it become? Is it your home state? Your country? The whole world?

Perhaps 'local' isn't even just a function of geography anymore, but a reference to the community we concern ourselves with.

What's local to you?

EGG, BEANSPROUTS AND GARLIC CHIVES

もやし入りニラ玉

THIS IS ONE OF OUR FAVOURITE DISHES. IT'S ECONOMICAL, SIMPLE AND ABSOLUTELY
DELICIOUS. ITS APPEAL COMES AS MUCH FROM ITS MARRIAGE OF TEXTURES AS IT DOES
FLAVOURS. SOFT, SILKY EGGS AND THREADS OF GARLIC CHIVES MEET CRUNCHY BEANSPROUTS
IN THE MOST PLEASANT WAY. BONITO FLAKES ARE A GREAT SEASONING FOR STIR-FRIED DISHES
AS THEY PROVIDE A STRONG SAVOURY ELEMENT WITHOUT ADDING EXCESS LIQUID TO A WOK OR PAN.

INGREDIENTS

2 tsp sesame oil, plus extra
   if needed
2 cups beansprouts
1 small bunch garlic chives,
   cut into 7cm lengths
½ tsp salt
2 tsp mirin
4 eggs, beaten
¼ cup bonito flakes

METHOD

1   Heat a wok or frying pan over high heat and add the sesame oil.
Fry the beansprouts and garlic chives with the salt and mirin until
softened. Move the vegetables to one side of the wok.

2   Add a little more oil if necessary then add the eggs and slowly
draw a spoon or spatula through them, creating folds as if making
an omelette. When nearly set but still quite runny, break up the
eggs, toss everything together and turn out onto a serving dish. The
eggs will continue to set off the heat. Top with the bonito flakes.

≫ You will get the most colour from your eggs if you beat them very well
so that the whites and yolks are completely mixed.

SERVES 2 **PREPARATION TIME** 5 MINS **COOKING TIME** 10 MINS

EGGPLANT NIBITASHI

ナスの煮浸し

A SIMPLY DRESSED DISH OF EGGPLANT IN A LIGHTLY SAVOURY DRESSING WILL BE A
WELCOME ADDITION TO ANY MEAL. IF YOU THINK ABOUT MANY OF THE SAUCES AND
DRESSINGS IN WESTERN CUISINES, THEY TEND TO BE SOUR LIKE A VINAIGRETTE OR
ADD A SEPARATE FLAVOUR LIKE A MUSHROOM OR RED WINE SAUCE. HERE, THE ROLE
OF THE DRESSING IS TO SEASON THE EGGPLANT AND ENHANCE ITS EXISTING
FLAVOUR, NOT TO MAKE IT TASTE LIKE SOMETHING ELSE.

INGREDIENTS

5 small Japanese eggplants
¼ cup Bonito Stock (page 30)
1 tbsp sake
2 tbsp soy sauce
½ tsp grated ginger
1 tbsp fine bonito flakes

METHOD

1 Cut a thin vertical slit only a few millimetres deep along the
length of each eggplant. This will allow steam to escape. Heat a grill
pan until very hot and roast the eggplants, turning frequently, for
about 20 minutes until their skins are blackened all over and the
eggplants feel soft to the touch. Plunge the eggplants into a bowl of
iced water and peel the skin from the flesh, leaving the caps intact,
then slice into large pieces. Drain well.

2 Bring the Bonito Stock, sake and soy sauce to a simmer. Pour
over the eggplants and garnish with a small pile of grated ginger
and another of fine bonito flakes.

≫ This can be served cold, at room temperature or even warm. Japanese
cuisine puts little emphasis on serving temperature for many dishes, as it
is often just a matter of personal preference.

SMALL DISH **PREPARATION TIME** 20 MINS **COOKING TIME** 25 MINS

BEANS IN BLACK SESAME

インゲン豆の胡麻よごし

THE DRESSING FOR THIS DISH SHOULD BE QUITE DRY. USE WHITE/GOLDEN SESAME SEEDS IF
YOU PREFER, OR SUBSTITUTE OTHER VEGETABLES. SPINACH OR ASPARAGUS WORK WELL.

INGREDIENTS

180g green beans

BLACK SESAME DRESSING
½ tbsp mirin
½ tbsp sake
½ tbsp soy sauce
¼ cup black sesame seeds

≫ Boiling the mirin and sake is
necessary to remove the raw burn
of alcohol.

METHOD

1 To make the black sesame dressing, bring the mirin and sake
to the boil in a small saucepan, then remove from the heat and add
the soy sauce. Toast the black sesame seeds (see page 103) and
grind in a mortar with a pestle. Add the liquid mixture, continuing to
grind to a thick paste.

2 Blanch the beans in boiling water for about a minute until just
tender but still a little crunchy, then drain and cut into 3cm lengths.
Drop into the sesame mixture, stirring and fanning to cool.

SMALL DISH **PREPARATION TIME** 10 MINS **COOKING TIME** 5 MINS

CORN WITH MAYONNAISE, BONITO AND NORI

焼きとうもろこしお好み焼き風

ONE OF THE MORE ODD COMBINATIONS IN MODERN JAPANESE COOKING IS THAT OF CORN AND
MAYONNAISE. YOU'LL FIND IT IN PIZZA, IN SALADS, TEMPURA OR EVEN MIXED INTO SUSHI.

INGREDIENTS

2 ears of corn, husks and
   strings removed
2 tbsp Japanese mayonnaise
1 tbsp bonito flakes
1 tsp aonori
½ tsp Korean chilli flakes

≫ The oil in the mayonnaise here
oils the corn much as butter would.

METHOD

1 Cut the corn into 5cm pieces and place into a dry frying pan
over low-medium heat. Cook for 15 minutes, turning frequently until
browned all over. Add the mayonnaise and continue turning until
the corn is glossy.

2 Remove the corn to a plate and scatter with the bonito flakes,
aonori and Korean chilli.

SERVES 4 **PREPARATION TIME** 5 MINS **COOKING TIME** 20 MINS

AGEDASHI TOFU

揚げ出し豆腐

AGEDASHI TOFU HAS CONVERTED COUNTLESS TOFU-HATERS INTO TOFU-LOVERS.
THE SLIGHTLY CRISP, SLIGHTLY STICKY FRIED COATING THAT BECOMES SILKY IN
THE SLIGHTLY SWEET STEEPING LIQUID IS PARTNERED BY SOME SHARP AND
SPICY TOPPINGS. IT MAKES YOU HUNGRY JUST THINKING ABOUT IT.

INGREDIENTS

¼ cup finely grated daikon
300g silken tofu
About 2 litres oil, for deep-
    frying
¼ cup potato starch, or
    cornflour
1 tbsp fine bonito flakes
2 thin spring onions, very finely
    sliced
½ tsp finely grated ginger
½ tsp shichimi togarashi, to
    serve

STEEPING LIQUID

⅓ cup Bonito Stock (page 30),
    or All-purpose Chicken Dashi
    (page 31)
1½ tbsp mirin
1½ tbsp soy sauce

METHOD

1 For the steeping liquid, bring the stock to a simmer in a small saucepan and add the mirin and soy sauce. Return to the simmer, then remove from the heat.

2 Place the finely grated daikon into a fine sieve to remove excess liquid.

3 To drain the tofu, turn it out of the packet onto a double layer of kitchen paper on a plate or board. Fold the paper to cover the top of the tofu and place a second plate on top. Allow to stand for 15 minutes as the weight of the top plate presses down the tofu. Trim the edges and cut into four blocks.

4 Heat the oil to 180°C. Carefully roll each of the tofu blocks in potato starch and fry for 3–4 minutes until puffed and crisp. Drain on a wire rack.

5 Arrange the tofu cubes in a deep bowl and place piles of the daikon, bonito flakes, spring onion and ginger on top. Pour the steeping liquid into the bowl around the edges, and sprinkle over a little of the shichimi togarashi. Serve immediately.

≫ Draining and pressing the tofu is very important for both flavour and texture. It will make it a little easier to handle, but you still have to be delicate with it.

SERVES 4, AS PART OF A SHARED MEAL **PREPARATION TIME** 30 MINS **COOKING TIME** 10 MINS

えぐい渋いも
味のうち

Egui shibui mo aji no uchi

Harshness and bitterness are parts of the taste.

We all like things to taste good, but do you ever stop to think about what good actually means? As children we're drawn to very simple, pleasant tastes. Candies that are unyieldingly sweet, and savoury treats heavy with salt.

As our palates develop we tend to crave more complexity in what we eat, and gain a greater appreciation of the meaning of flavour. Harshness and bitterness aren't often considered pleasant tastes, but they are some of the most important aspects of our food.

It's said that in a formal Japanese tea ceremony, the bitterness of green tea is a metaphor that causes the drinker to reflect on the bitterness of the world. That may be a romantic way of looking at it, but certainly the bitterness of drinks like tea and coffee is a big part of their appeal. Similarly, vegetables like bitter gourd (page 179) are prized for their bitter flavour. Squeeze out too much of the harsh liquid from a portion of grated daikon to serve with grilled fish and it becomes bland.

If we try to remove too much of the reality from our food, it becomes sanitised and boring. Particularly with vegetables where these kinds of harsh or bitter notes are often found, we need to be aware not to over-season foods to completely mask those kinds of tastes. After all, they're what gives our food character.

ODEN

おでん

ODEN IS ONE OF THE MOST DELICATE, ELEGANT AND UNIVERSALLY LOVED DISHES IN
JAPANESE CUISINE, AND FOR ME IT IS A REVELATION. SIMPLE INGREDIENTS SEASONED SO
GENTLY AS TO LAY EACH INDIVIDUAL CHARACTERISTIC BARE, BUT SO PERFECTLY AS TO
WANT FOR NOTHING ELSE. IT IS A PERFECT COMFORT FOOD.

INGREDIENTS

4 eggs
1 large daikon, peeled and
    halved into two long cylinders
    with a deep cross cut into one
    end of each cylinder
3 medium potatoes, peeled
    and halved
200g konnyaku
4 *satsuma-age* (fried fish
    cakes), halved
4 *ganmodoki* (fried vegetable
    tofu)
6 fish balls
2 pieces *hanpen* (white fish
    cakes)
2 *chikuwa* (cylindrical grilled
    fish cakes), halved on an
    angle
300g grilled tofu or firm tofu,
    cut into 5cm cubes
2 pieces kombu
1 tbsp *karashi* (Japanese
    mustard) or hot English
    mustard, to serve

BROTH

1.5 litres Bonito Stock (page 30)
½ cup sake
3 tsp salt
2 tbsp soy sauce

METHOD

1 Bring a pot of water to the boil and boil the eggs for 8 minutes,
then plunge into a bowl of cold water and peel.

2 Peel the daikon and potatoes and place whole into cold water
in a medium saucepan. Bring to the boil and boil for 5 minutes.

3 Cut the konnyaku into triangles and cut a cross-hatch pattern
into one side, running the knife about halfway into the konnyaku.
Place the konnyaku into a small saucepan of cold water and bring
to a rolling boil, boil the konnyaku for 5 minutes and then rinse well.

4 Place the fried fish cakes and *ganmodoki* in a flat strainer or
colander and pour boiling water over them to rinse off any surface
oil. Drain well. Thread the fish balls onto skewers.

5 Place the daikon, potatoes, eggs, konnyaku and kombu in a
pot with the stock, sake, salt and soy sauce. Bring to barely a
simmer, then reduce heat to very low. Add the tofu and *ganmodoki*
and heat slowly for 30 minutes. Add the various fish cakes and fish
balls and heat for a further 10 minutes. Turn off the heat, cover
the oden and allow it to sit for at least an hour or two to absorb the
seasoning. You can keep it warm throughout this process if you
like, or you can allow it to cool and reheat it later to serve.

6 Arrange the ingredients in a serving bowl and pour over as much
of the simmering broth as you like. Serve with the hot mustard.

≫ Oden is at its best when there are lots of different ingredients in the
pot, each subtly seasoning each other. Leave out especially strongly
flavoured or oily ingredients that could dominate others. Oden is like a
good conversation. Nobody should be shouting.

SERVES 4–8 **PREPARATION TIME** 30 MINS **COOKING TIME** 1 HOUR, PLUS 1–2 HOURS RESTING

CHILLED TOFU WITH TOMATO AND PONZU

冷奴のトマトポン酢がけ

TAKING A BLOCK OF SILKEN TOFU AND PAIRING ITS SOFT TEXTURE WITH A FLAVOURFUL
TOPPING IS COMMON IN CHINESE CUISINE, WHERE THE TOPPINGS ARE USUALLY STRONGLY
SAVOURY, LIKE FRIED ONIONS, GARLIC AND THICK SOY SAUCE, OR CHOPPED PRESERVED
CENTURY EGGS, BUT IN JAPAN THEY OFTEN TAKE A LIGHTER APPROACH, ADDING GRATED
GINGER AND BONITO FLAKES OR, AS IN THIS CASE, A FEW CHOPPED TOMATOES AND
A LIGHT PONZU DRESSING. IT'S INCREDIBLY REFRESHING.

INGREDIENTS

½ cup finely grated daikon
300g silken tofu, drained and
    pressed (see page 82)
½ cup cherry tomatoes,
    quartered
¼ cup Ponzu (page 102)
1 tbsp finely chopped chives

METHOD

1   Place the finely grated daikon in a fine sieve to remove excess
liquid. Trim the edges of the tofu and top with the cherry tomatoes
then the daikon. Pour over the Ponzu and scatter with the chives.

≫ Korean kimchi is also a popular topping for tofu in Japan – or try my
personal favourite, just some excellent quality tofu with a little mineral salt.

SERVES 4 AS PART OF A SHARED MEAL   **PREPARATION TIME** 10 MINS   **COOKING TIME** 0 MINS

CARROT AND LOTUS ROOT KINPIRA

人参とれんこんのきんぴら

KINPIRA IS NAMED AFTER A JAPANESE HERO OF LEGEND AND IT'S SAID THAT HIS
NAME WAS CHOSEN FOR THE DISH BECAUSE ITS BOLD, STRONG FLAVOUR IS REMINISCENT
OF HIS BOLDNESS AND STRENGTH. THE IDEA IS TO FRY THE VEGETABLES AND THEN ALLOW
THEM TO TOTALLY ABSORB THE SEASONINGS.

INGREDIENTS

1 small carrot
1 lotus root
1 tsp vinegar
1 tsp vegetable oil
2 tbsp Bonito Stock (page 30),
   or water
2 tbsp sake
1 tbsp mirin
2 tbsp soy sauce
2 tsp sugar
1 dried red chilli, sliced
½ tsp sesame oil
½ tsp toasted sesame seeds

METHOD

1   Peel the carrot and cut long vertical strips into it without cutting
through the stalk end. Pointing the carrot away from you, use a
knife to shave small strips from the carrot, like whittling a piece of
wood. Peel the lotus root, halve lengthways and slice into very thin
half-moons. If the lotus root is very slender, you may not need to
halve it before slicing (as pictured). Cover the sliced lotus root
with cold water in a bowl and add the vinegar. Allow to stand for
10 minutes then strain well.

2   Heat a wide saucepan or frying pan over high heat and add
the oil, lotus root and carrot. Fry for 2 minutes. Mix the stock, sake,
mirin, soy sauce, sugar and chilli, and add to the lotus root and
carrot. Bring to a simmer and simmer for about 8 minutes until
the liquid is completely evaporated. Transfer to a plate or bowl and
allow to cool to room temperature. To serve, drizzle over a little
sesame oil and scatter with sesame seeds.

≫ The style of cut used for the carrot is called *sasagaki*, meaning 'shaving
cuts'. It's used for creating thin slivers of mainly long, thin and firm
vegetables like carrot or burdock.

SERVES 4 AS PART OF A SHARED MEAL   **PREPARATION TIME** 20 MINS   **COOKING TIME** 10 MINS

VEGETABLE SKEWERS WITH MISO-DARE

味噌だれ野菜の串焼き

THE MORE CARE THAT GOES INTO PREPARING A MEAL, THE MORE SATISFYING IT CAN BE. KEEP THE VEGETABLES SEPARATE SO THAT YOU CAN APPRECIATE THE FLAVOUR OF EACH INDIVIDUALLY. VEGETABLES REALLY ARE WONDERFUL THINGS.

INGREDIENTS

VEGETABLES

2–4 Japanese eggplants, cut in half lengthways, with the skin cut in a crosshatch pattern

6–8 ears of baby corn, threaded onto 2 skewers

6–8 okra, threaded onto 2 skewers

1 onion, cut into thick rings and threaded onto a skewer

1 small sweet potato, cut into thick rings, halves or quarters, par-boiled and threaded onto a skewer

1 block firm tofu, drained and cut into thick single rectangles and threaded onto a skewer

8 fresh shiitake mushrooms, caps halved and stems trimmed, each skewered separately

2–3 thick spring onions or thin leeks, cut into 5cm batons and threaded onto a skewer

1 cup cherry tomatoes, threaded 3 to each skewer

Salt, for seasoning and to serve

1 tsp grated ginger, to serve

MISO-DARE

½ cup light miso

¼ cup sake

¼ cup mirin

2 tbsp sesame oil

½ cup Bonito Stock (page 30) or No. 1 Stock (page 30)

1 tbsp rice vinegar

METHOD

1 For the *miso-dare*, mix the miso with the sake, mirin and sesame oil to a smooth paste. Dilute with the stock and vinegar to a brushing consistency.

2 If the vegetables are very dry, spray or brush with a little water or oil and season with salt such that the salt sticks to the vegetables. If applying the *miso-dare* later, you can skip the seasoning step.

3 Grill the vegetables over coals or on a barbecue, turning regularly until tender. If cooking indoors, fry the vegetables in a very small amount of oil in a large frying pan.

4 For some of the vegetables, but not all, brush with a little of the *miso-dare* and continue to grill until the miso is lightly toasted and fragrant. The *miso-dare* is particularly good with tofu, sweet potato and Japanese eggplant.

5 Serve the vegetable skewers with a little extra salt and a small pile of grated ginger.

≫ The *miso-dare* can be kept in the fridge for a few weeks, ready for another round of grilled, barbecued or baked vegetables.

SERVES 2–4 **PREPARATION TIME** 20 MINS **COOKING TIME** 30 MINS

SIMMERED NEW POTATOES

小芋の煮物

UNDERSTANDING THIS SIMMERING PROCESS IS THE WEAPON YOU NEED TO HAVE IN YOUR ARSENAL IF YOU WANT TO COOK JAPANESE CUISINE. IT CAN BE APPLIED TO ALMOST ANY VEGETABLE (OR MEAT OR FISH, OR MIXTURE OF THEM FOR THAT MATTER). THE IDEA IS NOT SO MUCH TO CREATE A MEAL, BUT A DISH THAT PRESENTS THAT INGREDIENT AT ITS MOST FLAVOURFUL, LIGHTLY SEASONED BY THE REDUCED SIMMERING LIQUID. THE CHALLENGE WITH THIS PROCESS IS GETTING THE AMOUNT OF LIQUID RIGHT. USE AS SMALL A POT AS YOU CAN TO JUST BARELY FIT ALL THE POTATOES (A SINGLE LAYER WOULD BE PREFERABLE) AND ADD AS LITTLE OF THE SIMMERING STOCK AS YOU HAVE TO. THE IDEA IS THAT THE LIQUID REDUCES IN THE SIMMERING PROCESS AND INTENSIFIES THE FLAVOUR.

INGREDIENTS

1 tsp sesame oil
400g new potatoes, peeled
500ml No. 1 Stock (page 30),
   or Bonito Stock (page 30)
2 tsp caster sugar
2 tsp sake
1 tbsp mirin
1 tbsp soy sauce

METHOD

1   Heat the sesame oil in a small saucepan over medium heat and add the potatoes, tossing to coat in the oil. Add enough of the stock to just barely cover the potatoes and bring to a simmer, then add the sugar, sake, mirin and soy sauce. Stir and cover with a drop lid or cartouche and simmer for 10 minutes. Remove the drop lid or cartouche, stir gently and simmer for a further 10 minutes until the liquid is reduced by about half and the potatoes are tender. (Test for tenderness with a sharp knife. Once inserted into the potato, the knife tip should come out very easily.) Allow the potatoes to cool to room temperature in the remaining liquid.

≫ These kinds of dishes can be served at room temperature or warm, as is your preference. If serving warm, allow the potatoes to cool in the liquid first to absorb the seasoning, then reheat them to serve.

SERVES 4 AS PART OF A SHARED MEAL **PREPARATION TIME** 15 MINS **COOKING TIME** 30 MINS

chapter semi-nine sweets

Japan has a long tradition of sweet making. In my other books and TV series, I've written and spoken about *wagashi*, traditional sweets made in a thousand varieties, from the impressionist jewels of *namagashi*, capturing tiny vignettes of the Japanese seasons for a tea ceremony, to *dagashi*, simple candy-store sweets to bring a smile to children's faces.

In this chapter I want to touch on *yogashi*, sweets of foreign origin that have been incorporated into Japanese cuisine. More often than not, as these sweets are brought into Japanese cuisine, they are made less sweet than their original inspiration, more in keeping with the Japanese palate. They are some of my favourite to eat, from green tea cakes (page 217) to puddings made with pumpkin (page 218), as the mildness better allows us to appreciate the flavours of fruits and other ingredients, unmasked by an oppressive blanket of saccharine sweetness.

OKINAWAN SALTED SHORTBREAD

ちんすこう

THE TINY ISLANDS THAT MAKE UP THE TROPICAL PARADISE OF OKINAWA ARE SOME OF MY
FAVOURITE DESTINATIONS IN JAPAN. THE PACE OF LIFE, THE WEATHER, THE BEAUTY AND OF
COURSE THE FOOD MAKE THEM A GREAT PLACE TO VISIT. OKINAWA IS KNOWN FOR MANY THINGS –
THE BIRTHPLACE OF KARATE; A UNIQUE FUSION CUISINE THAT BLENDS SOUTHEAST ASIA, CHINA,
THE US AND JAPAN; AND EXTREMELY HIGH QUALITY PRODUCE, FROM PORK TO BITTER GOURDS
TO SEAWEEDS. TWO OF ITS MOST FAMOUS EXPORTS ARE A RICH, BLACK SUGAR CALLED *KOKUTOU*
AND MINERAL-RICH SEA SALTS. OF COURSE, IF YOU CAN GET THOSE PRODUCTS FROM OKINAWA,
MORE'S THE BETTER, BUT OTHERWISE ANY DARK BROWN SUGAR AND SEA SALT FLAKES WILL DO.

INGREDIENTS

80g lard or vegetable
  shortening
60g soft dark brown sugar
150g plain flour
1 tsp sea salt flakes

METHOD

1 Heat your oven to 160°C. In a medium saucepan, heat the
lard and brown sugar together over low heat until liquid and
combined. Add the flour and mix to a soft dough. Roll the dough
between two sheets of baking paper to around 1cm thick and
cut into 8cm x 3cm batons (using a crinkle cutter if possible).

2 Transfer the biscuits to a baking sheet and scatter with sea salt,
lightly pressing it into the top of the biscuit.

3 Bake for around 25 minutes until firm. Allow to cool before serving.

≫ The addition of salt helps us appreciate complexity in sweetness.
Just think of the richness of salted caramel. When I was young, my
grandmother used to sprinkle salt on under-ripe fruits to make them
taste more sweet.

MAKES ABOUT 20 **PREPARATION TIME** 20 MINS **COOKING TIME** 25 MINS

FRUIT JELLIES

フルーツ寒天

KANTEN IS MORE POPULARLY KNOWN OUTSIDE JAPAN AS AGAR AGAR. IT'S A SEAWEED
BASED GELLING AGENT BUT ITS PROPERTIES ARE VERY DIFFERENT TO GELATINE. THE JELLIES
IT PRODUCES ARE FIRMER AND CRUNCHIER. KANTEN HAS BEEN USED FOR MAKING JAPANESE
SWEETS FOR HUNDREDS OF YEARS. HERE, A LIGHTLY SWEETENED WATER JELLY ENCASES
DELICIOUS COLOURFUL FRUITS. OUR KIDS LOVE THESE.

INGREDIENTS

Various fruits, such as
strawberries, blueberries,
lychees (tinned is fine),
mandarin, kiwifruit,
rockmelon
1 litre water
120g caster sugar
8g kanten (agar agar) powder
(or according to packet
directions)

METHOD

1   Prepare the fruit by cutting into bite-sized pieces, large
chunks, decorative cuts or shapes. A variety of shapes, colours
and sizes is good.

2   Combine the water, sugar and kanten in a medium saucepan
and whisk over medium heat until the kanten and sugar are
dissolved. Allow to cool until just warm to the touch but not set.
You don't want to cook the fruit.

3   Pour into a 1.5 litre capacity mould (e.g. a 20cm square cake
tin) and press the fruits into the liquid. Allow to cool until set, then
refrigerate until chilled. You may find it easier to line the mould but if
you do, line it with baking paper, as plastic wrap may leave shapes
in the base of the jellies. Carefully turn out the jellies and cut into
individual cubes. Alternatively, set the jellies in individual moulds.
Individual moulds will make it easier to keep the fruits separated.

≫ You need to follow the directions on the packet of the kanten if there
are any. Brands may differ in their setting strength.

MAKES ABOUT 16 JELLIES **PREPARATION TIME** 30 MINS **COOKING TIME** 10 MINS, PLUS 4 HOURS CHILLING TIME

FRUIT PARFAITS

フルーツ・パフェ

THESE FRUIT PARFAITS MAY LOOK IMPRESSIVE BUT THEY'RE ACTUALLY VERY EASY TO MAKE,
WHICH MAKES THEM MY KIND OF SWEET. YOU DON'T NEED ANY SPECIAL EQUIPMENT LIKE ICE-CREAM
MAKERS OR JUICERS – JUST A FREEZER, A WHISK AND SOME GOOD FRUIT IN SEASON.

INGREDIENTS

1kg each fruit in season
  (see suggestions below)
2 cups good quality vanilla
  ice-cream, optional
Mint, baby herbs or citrus rind,
  to garnish

GRANITA

¼ cup caster sugar
¾ cup water
1 cup puréed fruit

YOGHURT CREAM

300ml thickened cream
300ml thick yoghurt

METHOD

1   For each 1kg peeled and deseeded fruit: purée and strain 250g, finely chop a further 250g and slice the remaining 500g.

2   To make the granita, mix the sugar and water together in a small saucepan and bring to a simmer, stirring to dissolve the sugar completely. Allow to cool to room temperature then stir through the puréed fruit. Freeze for at least 4 hours or until solid.

3   To make the yoghurt cream, whip the cream to soft peaks then fold through the yoghurt. Chill until ready to assemble.

4   Chill your parfait glasses and assemble as follows, or just arrange the layers to your preference:
A layer of sliced fruit in the base of the glass
A layer of yoghurt cream
A layer of diced fruit
Another layer of yoghurt cream
A mound of granita
A scoop of ice-cream, if using
Herbs or citrus rind, to garnish.

FRUIT SUGGESTIONS

Here are some of my favourite fruit and garnish combinations, as pictured:

‣   Honeydew melon and green and red seedless grapes, topped with shiso cress
‣   White peach and mango, topped with strips of lime rind
‣   Strawberry, raspberry and blueberry topped with chervil
‣   Orange and apricot with vanilla ice-cream.

≫ This is great for afternoon tea with friends or even a dinner party dessert as you can make all the elements in advance and then just assemble them as needed.

SERVES 4 **PREPARATION TIME** 25 MINS **COOKING TIME** 5 MINS, PLUS 4 HOURS FREEZING

砂糖食いの
若死

Sato kui no wakajini

Eat sugar and die young.

It may sound terribly macabre, but the dark message of this proverb is really a call to moderation, and a warning against excess. Sugar here is used as a metaphor for all decadent things, sweet or otherwise.

It's almost incongruous for a nation so devoted to the pursuit of excellence in food to be so cautious of the indulgence of it. Temperance in Japanese cuisine is not simply a matter of wellbeing, but an aesthetic. If we indulge ourselves constantly or even frequently, doesn't the act of indulgence itself lose its meaning?

There is as much appeal in the austerity of a bowl of rice and a plate of pickles as there is in the most elaborate of sweet confections. And yet in the balance of all things neither, without the other, would be as appealing.

GREEN TEA ROLL CAKE

抹茶ロールケーキ

THE DIFFERENCE BETWEEN THIS STYLE OF CAKE AND A SWISS ROLL – GREEN TEA AND LACK OF JAM ASIDE – IS THE SINGLE FAT BOLT OF CREAM THAT RUNS DOWN THE CENTRE. PURISTS MAY LOVE THE SPIRAL SWIRL OF A TRADITIONAL SWISS ROLL BUT I REALLY THINK JAPAN IS ON TO SOMETHING HERE.

INGREDIENTS

3 eggs, separated
60g caster sugar
Pinch of salt
1 tsp rice vinegar
¼ cup grapeseed oil
80g plain flour or low-gluten
    flour
2 tbsp matcha powder

FILLING

300ml thickened cream
2 tbsp icing sugar, plus extra
    for dusting
1 vanilla bean, scraped

METHOD

1   Heat your oven to 200°C. Beat the egg whites to soft peaks then add half the caster sugar, the salt and vinegar and beat to firm peaks.

2   Cream the egg yolks and sugar until pale and doubled in volume. Beat in the oil and then gently mix through the flour and matcha powder. Add one-third of the meringue and mix well, then add the remaining two-thirds and fold through gently until the batter is completely uniform.

3   For the filling, beat the cream, sugar and vanilla until firm. Refrigerate until ready to use.

4   Spread the cake batter gently into a lined 20cm x 30cm baking tin and bake for 15 minutes. Allow to cool, then remove from the pan and place onto a sheet of plastic wrap. Spread the filling over the cake and mound it in the centre in a long line. Roll the cake so it is barely touching at the base. Secure with the plastic wrap and refrigerate for at least 30 minutes. Slice and serve.

≫ Thickened cream contains gelatine which, when the cake is chilled, will help it to hold its structure. Still, use a sharp knife when cutting to stop the filling from squeezing out like toothpaste from a tube.

MAKES 1 CAKE   **PREPARATION TIME** 30 MINS   **COOKING TIME** 15 MINS, PLUS 30 MINUTES COOLING

PUMPKIN PUDDING

かぼちゃプリン

I LOVE USING PUMPKIN AS A SWEET INGREDIENT. IT HAS A LOVELY VELVETY TEXTURE AND ADDS A BIT OF CHARACTER BEYOND THE CLINICAL SWEETNESS OF WHITE SUGAR. A FEW PEOPLE I ASKED DURING THE TESTING OF THIS RECIPE DIDN'T THINK THAT IT NEEDED THE CINNAMON-DUSTED CREAM. MAYBE IT DOESN'T, BUT THEN AGAIN, MAYBE IT DOES...

INGREDIENTS

400g Jap or Kent pumpkin, or Japanese kabocha, peeled and cut into chunks
1 can evaporated milk
3 eggs plus 4 egg yolks
1 can condensed milk
½ tsp vanilla extract
½ cup sugar
300ml double cream, to serve (optional)
Cinnamon, to serve

METHOD

1 Bring a large pot of water to the boil and boil the pumpkin for 12 minutes until very tender. Drain well and blend to a purée with the evaporated milk.

2 Beat the eggs and egg yolks and whisk in the condensed milk, pumpkin purée and vanilla extract. Try not to incorporate too much air into the mixture or it will create bubbles in the pudding.

3 Heat your oven to 180°C. Heat the sugar in a small saucepan over medium heat until it becomes a dark caramel. Pour the caramel into the base of a rectangular loaf tin and let it harden. Pour the pumpkin custard mixture on top of the caramel.

4 Place the loaf tin on top of a wet tea towel inside a larger baking dish in the oven. Pour boiling water into the larger baking dish until it comes halfway up the side of the loaf tin. Bake for 45 minutes to 1 hour, until the pudding is just barely cooked through to the centre. Check doneness by tapping the edge of the loaf tin. Tapping will create a ripple on the top of the custard where it is not set.

5 Allow to cool to room temperature and then chill in the fridge for at least 1 hour. Turn out, cut thick slices and top with a little cream, if using, and sprinkled cinnamon.

≫ You can make this pudding in individual ramekins just as for a crème caramel if you prefer to serve it that way, or even set them in small jars to dig into instead of turning them out.

SERVES 6–8 **PREPARATION TIME** 30 MINS **COOKING TIME** 1 HOUR 30 MINUTES

FRUIT SANDWICHES

フルーツサンド

IN JAPAN YOU CAN FIND THESE LITTLE FRUIT SANDWICHES IN JUST ABOUT ANY CONVENIENCE STORE.
THEY'RE A BIT LIKE A HEALTHIER VERSION OF A STRAWBERRY SHORTCAKE.

INGREDIENTS

8 slices very soft Japanese-
   style white bread, or brioche
Strawberries, kiwifruit,
   mandarins, sliced

SWEETENED YOGHURT CREAM

300ml thickened cream
50g icing sugar, or to your taste
300ml thick yoghurt

METHOD

1 Whip the cream and icing sugar to firm peaks and fold
through the thick yoghurt.

2 Spread 4 slices of bread with a thick layer of the yoghurt
cream and press the fruit slices into it. Cover the fruit with more
yoghurt cream ensuring there are no air pockets, then top each
slice with the remaining bread. Smooth the edges of the cream,
cover with plastic wrap, and refrigerate for at least 15 minutes
to firm the cream.

3 Using a very, very sharp knife, cut through the sandwiches
to first remove the crusts to expose a cross-section of the fruit
and cream filling, then to halve each sandwich into two smaller
finger sandwiches.

≫ Use a very, very sharp, non-serrated knife to cut the sandwiches.
If the knife is not sharp enough, its pressure on the bread or the fruit
will squeeze the cream out of the centre.

SERVES 4 FOR AFTERNOON TEA **PREPARATION TIME** 15 MINS, PLUS 15 MINS CHILLING TIME **COOKING TIME** 0 MINS

MILLE-CREPE

ミルクレープ

I MUST CONFESS A TERRIBLE WEAKNESS FOR THIS CAKE. AT CAFES AROUND JAPAN IT COMES IN MANY DIFFERENT VARIETIES, WITH BATTER OR CREAMS FLAVOURED WITH GREEN TEA OR COFFEE, OR DRIZZLED WITH CARAMEL, OR SANDWICHED WITH FRUIT, BUT I LIKE THE SIMPLICITY OF THE ORIGINAL. IT'S VERY DENSE AND RICH, SO YOU DON'T NEED A LOT OF IT, BUT IT MAKES A FANTASTIC TREAT.

INGREDIENTS

1.3kg flour
2 litres milk
12 eggs
½ cup icing sugar, plus extra
  for dusting
1 tsp salt
125g butter, melted, plus 50g
  extra for brushing

FILLING

600ml thickened cream
1 tsp vanilla extract
60g icing sugar

METHOD

1 Place the flour, milk, eggs, icing sugar and salt together in a blender and blend until smooth. You may need to do this in batches. Rest in the fridge for 30 minutes, then whisk in the melted butter.

2 Heat a perfectly flat 24cm frying pan or crepe pan and brush with a little melted butter. Tilt the pan and add about 2 tbsp batter, quickly swirling the batter to completely coat the pan in a thin layer. Cook for about 2 minutes until lightly browned, then flip and cook the other side for about 20 seconds until set. Remove to a plate to cool. Repeat for the remaining batter to make about 15 crepes.

3 For the filling, beat the cream, vanilla and sugar together until soft peaks form. Chill in the fridge for 10 minutes.

4 To assemble the cake, spread a crepe with a thin layer of the cream to around the same thickness as the crepe itself. Take special care that the cream goes all the way to the edges, and it is the same thickness as the cream at the centre. Place another crepe on top, spread with cream and repeat the process until all the crepes are used, finishing with a crepe on top. Chill in the fridge for at least 30 minutes. Dust the top of the cake with icing sugar, then slice and serve.

≫ If you have two crepe pans of identical size, you can make two at a time to really speed up the process. It's worth thinking about when buying pans for crepes or pancakes. Nobody should be kept waiting too long for pancakes.

SERVES 8–10 **PREPARATION TIME** 1 HOUR, PLUS 70 MINUTES RESTING **COOKING TIME** 30 MINUTES

A RECIPE THAT IS AS SIMPLE AS CUTTING UP AN APPLE MIGHT SEEM ALMOST INSULTINGLY BASIC IN A COOKBOOK YOU'VE SPENT YOUR HARD-EARNED MONEY ON, BUT I'VE CHOSEN THIS AS THE LAST RECIPE HERE BECAUSE IT'S THE MOST IMPORTANT IN THIS WHOLE BOOK.

I travelled the entire length of Japan a few years ago – from the top of Hokkaido to the islands of Okinawa – and passing through Nagoya around halfway through my trip, I spoke to a miso producer who was making miso in the traditional Nagoya style: steamed soybeans and koji fermenting in huge oak barrels weighted down with stones from the centre of a fast flowing river (where they are the smoothest and heaviest, as the speed of the water washes away anything rough or light).

Our conversation turned to apples, and I told him how much I love Japanese apples. They're huge and perfect and almost candy-sweet.

'Oh no!' he exclaimed. 'They're awful!' What I loved about them, he absolutely hated. He found them too sweet and juicy, without personality and character. They were nothing like the apples he had as a child which were sometimes sour, sometimes rotten, but when you got a really sweet one it was a moment to remember. You'd tell the whole family and maybe even share them with your neighbours. When every supermarket now stocks the same perfect, uniform apples, it's harder to build memories around them.

I have dozens of memories around apples. My grandmother used to cut them for me after dinner, carefully peeling them and taking out the cores and dividing them into perfect little segments on a brown melamine plate for me to eat, sitting cross-legged on our scratchy brown sofa.

When we first started living together, Asami would cut apples for me just like my grandmother did, and although it's strange to think so, that feeling of familiarity is probably part of the reason we ended up getting married.

These days, I cut little rabbit apples for our children, and they love them. When they're a little older I'll show them how to cut these themselves and one day they'll cut them for their children. Every apple they cut will teach them a little more about how to choose a good piece of fruit, how to use a knife, and why an apple is better for their health than a chocolate bar or ice-cream. They might even end up loving the taste of a simple apple as much as their father does.

A recipe like this is the very beginning of a lifelong relationship with food. Such a simple and wonderful thing that it is.

RABBIT APPLES

ウサギりんご

INGREDIENTS

A very good red-skinned apple

METHOD

1 Cut the apple into thin wedges. Using a sharp knife, cut just through the skin, creating a 'V' such that the point ends about 1cm from the end of the wedge. Make a single cut from the opposite end of the wedge all the way to about ½ cm from the end where the point of the 'V' sits. The skin of the apple should fall away to reveal a rabbit ears shape. Cut away the core, so that the wedge now resembles a rabbit bounding over a field.

SERVES EVERYONE **PREPARATION TIME** 5 MINS **COOKING TIME** 0 MINS

INDEX

The best thing about cookbooks in the digital age is that this isn't the end. You can find lots more recipes, as well as videos, tips and hints on my social media accounts. Please get in touch. I'd be happy to answer any of your questions.

www.adamliaw.com

 adamliaw

 adamliaw

 AdamLiawFanPage

 adamliaw

 hachette
AUSTRALIA

Published in Australia and New Zealand in 2016
by Hachette Australia
(an imprint of Hachette Australia Pty Limited)
Level 17, 207 Kent Street, Sydney NSW 2000
www.hachette.com.au

10 9 8 7 6 5 4 3 2 1

National Library of Australia
Cataloguing-in-Publication data:

Liaw, Adam, author.

The Zen kitchen / Adam Liaw.

978 0 7336 3431 4 (hardback)

Cooking, Japanese.

641.5952

Jacket and internal design by Liz Seymour/Seymour Designs
Photography by Steve Brown
Food styling by Berni Smithies
Food preparation by Olivia Andrews
Typeset in 10/14 Trade Gothic by Seymour Designs
Colour reproduction by Splitting Image
Printed in China by Toppan Leefung Printing Limited